# *Independent B*
## *Shropshir*

CW00338324

## Neville Mercer

© 2011 Venture Publications Ltd

**ISBN 978 1905 304 417**

All rights reserved. Except for normal review purposes no part of this book maybe reproduced or utilised in any form by any means, electrical or mechanical, including photocopying, recording or by an information storage and retrieval system, without the prior written consent of Venture Publications Ltd., Glossop, Derbyshire.

*Computer Origination, Design and Layout by Mark Senior*

# Contents

(Front Cover) WS Yeates provided the bodywork for a variety of AEC Reliances but for only one Tiger Cub. Delivered in 1958 to The Delaine of Bourne, MTL 750 passed to Vagg of Knockin Heath in January 1970 and is currently preserved in the Leicester area. (B Mel Gough Collection)

(Back Cover) KNT 780 was among the last Royal Tigers built for the domestic market and was equipped with Burlingham Seagull bodywork for the Gittins brothers of Crickheath. It was sold to Vagg of Knockin Heath after the Gittins retired and was later acquired by Boulton of Cardington (as seen here) for use on heritage services. (Malcolm Yeomans)

(Title Page) There is no evidence that this vehicle ever saw service on Salopia's local bus network, but who could resist including it in a book about Shropshire independents? Foden PVFE6 observation coach GUJ 243 is seen at the premises of coachbuilder James Whitson before delivery to Whitchurch in September 1950. (Author's Collection)

# INTRODUCTION

Until 1974, when Conservative Prime Minister Edward Heath took his monumentally unpopular decision to modify or abolish many of the traditional political boundaries, there were 42 counties in England. From Lower Mosley Street bus station in Manchester (or the adjacent East Street coach station favoured by independent operators) it was possible to reach destinations in 35 of those counties by direct express coach services. This impressive total included every English county within a 75 mile radius bar one. The solitary exception was the county of Shropshire, relatively close in terms of mileage and yet so far away from a logistical viewpoint.

For a bus enthusiast this lack of a direct coach link presented problems. As a purist I believed that trains were for train-spotters and avoided them whenever humanly possible, and yet Shropshire had more than its share of attractions. Fellow enthusiasts brought back tales of a county where Midland Red's nominal hegemony was challenged by dozens of small independents, where bonneted Bedfords were still an everyday commonplace, and where limited production marques such as Sentinel could be found operating in direct competition with BMMO's vaguely Stalinist homebuilds on busy urban bus routes. By the end of 1965 I was more than ready for an adventure into the unknown and decided that Oswestry would be my first target during the upcoming Christmas school holidays.

My informants among the Lower Mosley Street bus-watching fraternity revealed that Wednesday (one of the town's two market days) would be the ideal choice and that the operators to be seen would include several small Welsh independents as well as the more locally based firms of Gittins, Hampson, Hyde, Parish, and Vagg. They also advised that reaching Oswestry by train was a fairly simple matter, but this information was duly ignored. Being a dogmatic bus-user led me to a bottom-numbing alternative involving a North Western Renown to Northwich (reached at 10.54 hours), a Crosville Lodekka from there to Chester (12.14), and then further Lodekka rides, first to Wrexham and then to Oswestry, finally arriving at around 14.30. This itinerary gave me just over an hour and a half in Oswestry before boarding

my fourth Crosville double-decker of the day for the first leg of the return journey. Perhaps someone out there can tell me why the interiors of Crosville's Lodekkas always smelled of burning oil while those of other Tilling group companies didn't. I certainly noticed the phenomenon during this lengthy expedition. In the same amount of travelling time I could have gone to London and back on North Western's newly introduced X5Z motorway service (and the fares involved would have been similar) but as I returned to my parents' doorstep just before 21.00 there was no doubt in my mind that my choice of destination had been the right one.

Chester had, as always, been a disappointment apart from municipal Foden PVD6s and Guy Arabs and a visiting Southdown Cavalier, but Wrexham had produced more than its share of local independents and provided a fitting hors d'oeuvre before the main course of the day. Among the delights on offer around Oswestry town centre were one of Vagg's two all-Leyland PD2s and a brace of their (ex-Eastern National) Bristol SC4LKs, Bedford OB/Duple Vistas from Gittins of Crickheath, Hyde of Ellesmere and Hughes of Llansilin, Parish's 1951 vintage Bedford SB/Duple Vega KWX 807, and both of Hampson's 'private-hire RF' Regal IVs which looked far more exotic in maroon than they had in their original London Transport livery. Some of Crosville's older single-deckers were also present but were easy to ignore given the tastier items on the metaphorical plate.

The early months of 1966 included further pioneering (for me) trips to Shrewsbury and Telford New Town. Shrewsbury was reached by North Western Y-type (to Newcastle-under-Lyme), PMT 'Jubilee Class' Reliance (to Market Drayton where Butter's Albion Victor/Harrington coach KEL 967 was an unexpected treat), and then a Midland Red S17 which passed the RAF bases at Ternhill and Shawbury on its way to the county town. In Shrewsbury's Barker Street bus station and the nearby parking areas I found assorted Vagg vehicles (including their other PD2), Valley Motor Services' impressive Tiger Cub with rare Mann Egerton Sandringham bodywork, Worthen Motorways Bedford-powered Commer Avenger CEP 168, Salopia's SB5/Duple Midland bus YAW 166, OB/Vistas from Boulton of Cardington and the Minsterley Motor Company, and two very welcome 'foreigners' in the shape of Mid-Wales Motorways' SB5/Yeates Pegasus PEP 380 and Sentinel STC4 GNT 961 – the latter vehicle already 16 years old and destined for another three years of service before its unfortunate destruction in a depot fire along with many other treasures. Another pleasant surprise was provided by the discovery of the Corvedale Motor Company's (ex-LT) Guy Vixen Special MXX 343 parked alongside the River Severn, apparently on a private-hire despite a hand-written cardboard destination sign proclaiming 'Tenbury Wells'.

Two weeks later it was Telford's turn, a journey involving another North Western Y-type (this time to Stafford), a leisurely ride on a GH Austin and Co Tiger Cub to Newport (with a long enough pause at Woodseaves to 'check out' their depot yard), and then a soon to be withdrawn BMMO S13 for the final connection to Wellington. This old established market town was famous for many years for its delightfully ramshackle bus station, manufactured from surplus gas-pipes, corrugated iron, and disintegrating paving stones. Although this facility did little to promote a modern image for the local bus industry it provided a perfect back-drop for the vehicles of the Telford independents. Within an hour of my arrival in the town my notebook had recorded two Sentinel SLC4s of Browns Coachways (one of them displaying 'schools service' in its eyebrow blind aperture despite my visit taking place on a Saturday), Priory Motor Services' unusual SBG/Strachan Everest 457 EMC, Smiths Eagle's Reliance/Burlingham bus NUX 256 and Daimler CVD6/Metalcraft coach DUX 655, Martlew's Bedford VAL14/Duple Midland bus 3170 NT, and Cooper's brand-new VAM5/Willowbrook bus FAW 156D. On subsequent trips to Telford I made time to visit the various operators' garages, revealing many more interesting vehicles rarely glimpsed in service.

These expeditions to Oswestry, Shrewsbury, and Telford all took place when I was 12 years old, so (realistically) it would have been impossible for me to reach the area much earlier. Age considerations aside, this was also the year when I made the move from pocket-money to my first part-time job and as a result extended trips of this nature became economically feasible. Nevertheless, the fleet histories and photographs collected over the following four and a half decades

have made me wish many times over that my date of birth had been in 1943 rather than 1953. By 1965/66 many of the rarest vehicles in Shropshire had already gone, among them such Oswestry celebrities as Lloyd's STL double-deckers and Vagg's Churchill-bodied Thornycroft coach EUJ 787, Shrewsbury regulars including Boulton's Crossley/Whitson EUJ 666, and a host of Telford superstars ranging from Browns Coachways trio of Vulcan 6PFs and Cooper's fleet of fully-fronted Crossleys to Hoggins' immaculate Plaxton-bodied Morris Commercial JMU 297. Diversity was at the heart of Shropshire's attraction to the bus enthusiast, and it inevitably diminished year-by-year as older vehicles finally fell to bits and were replaced by newer and more standardised equipment. This process quickened from 1968 onwards as government grants became available and the remaining relics from the 1940s and 1950s gave way to a flood of Willowbrook-bodied Bedford VAMs and their Ford equivalents. Browns Coachways were the last of the Telford operators to succumb to this sea-change, maintaining their famous fleet of Sentinels until 1971 when several of the vehicles were more than 20 years old. The story of the bus industry in Shropshire was about so much more than the Midland Red monopoly suggested by area agreement maps.

# Border Country

In terms of acreage the traditional county of Shropshire was one of the largest in England, but also one of the most sparsely populated with just over 300,000 inhabitants by the middle of the twentieth century. The vast majority of these residents were concentrated in Shrewsbury and a dozen or so small market towns scattered around the county, resulting in an even lower population density than might have been expected in rural areas. As a result public services, including transport, were intrinsically difficult to provide. On the other hand, the wide open spaces between settlements were attractive to a variety of interests, the lowland areas favoured by farmers and the hills by the tourist trade. There were also deposits of valuable natural resources, including iron and coal, to be found within the county's boundaries.

In earlier times would-be invaders ranging from the Roman Empire to the Anglo-Saxons and the Normans had found it difficult territory to conquer (and even harder to secure) due to

In the pre-war era vehicles of Ford, Chevrolet and Bedford manufacture formed a clear majority of the local bus and coach population. Despite its Shropshire registration this Waveney bodied Bedford WHB, UJ 9058, is technically an intruder as it belonged to Hailstone of Churchstoke, a few hundred yards across the county boundary in Montgomeryshire. (Omnibus Society)

William Swain was a pioneer in the development of bus services in the hilly terrain to the south of Shrewsbury. His final new vehicle, AUJ 139, was a Duple bodied Bedford WTB bus, seen here at its destination. Note the RW Carpenter Bedford OWB parked behind it. The Swain business would later metamorphose into the Minsterley Motor Co. (Omnibus Society)

RW (Bob) Carpenter was another early operator of services to the south of Shrewsbury. This Pickering-bodied Daimler CP6, VD 1524, joined the fleet during the war and came from Central SMT in Scotland. (Omnibus Society)

And here is another Carpenter vehicle with Scottish connections despite its Stockport registration. Leyland TS2 Tiger DB 9311 was new to North Western with a 26-seat Leyland coach body, but soon passed to W Alexander & Son who rebodied it as a 32-seater in their own bodyworks. Just before the war it was sold to Rose of Bishops Castle and was then acquired, with the rest of that business, by Bob Carpenter. (Omnibus Society via Tim Butler)

frequent incursions by Welsh warlords who saw themselves, with some justification, as the native masters of the southern half of Great Britain. This led to the construction of the massive defensive earthwork known as Offa's Dyke in the eighth century, named after the reigning monarch of the Kingdom of Mercia. The area was eventually subjugated during the fourteenth century by the appointment of an aristocratic class known as the Marcher Lords, among them the Fitzalan and Mortimer families, who acted as the local viceroys of the English crown and commanded private armies from their border region fortresses.

Six hundred years later a Birmingham-based (but London controlled) bus company would also find itself unable to exercise any convincing dominion over these western marches of its titular realm. The very first motor-bus services into Shropshire were operated by the Great Western Railway, which opened a route from Wolverhampton to Bridgnorth in November 1904. The initial equipment, a trio of Clarkson steam-buses, proved to be less capable than imagined and was replaced by a similar number of petrol-powered Milnes-Daimlers and Durkopps in January 1905. When the GWR eventually decided to abandon this route in June 1923 it was sold, not to Midland Red as might have been expected, but to Wolverhampton Corporation who continued to operate it until the 1973 route swaps between Midland Red and the reconstituted West Midlands PTE. The very first bus route into Shropshire thus became one of the last to be acquired by Midland Red before its ultimate dismemberment into five smaller companies.

In more rural areas it can be difficult to ascertain the exact point at which individual village carriers either retired in the face of competition from the internal combustion engine or took the decision to exchange their horses and carts for motorised lorry-buses, but by 1908 the area of north-eastern Shropshire around the market town of Whitchurch was already blessed by a network of independent bus services run by Ellis Chesworth, initially with a single Commer. In 1934 the business (which used the appropriate name of Pioneer Motor Service) was sold to JR Richards and Sons of Whitchurch, a company better known by its later trading-name of Salopia Saloon Coaches.

Chesworth's original garage had actually been situated in Bronington, just across the Welsh border

in Flintshire, and the next contender to appear on the scene was also from an adjacent county. The Worcestershire Motor Transport company began a regular service from its Kidderminster base to Cleobury Mortimer in southern Shropshire in late 1913. In October 1914 many of WMT's vehicles were requisitioned for military use and the company was forced to transfer several of its services (including that to Cleobury) to BMMO. The route became Midland Red's first foothold in Shropshire. Meanwhile, back in the north of the county, there were other intruders. Wrexham and District started market-day services from its home-town in Denbighshire to both Oswestry and Ellesmere in the Spring of 1915, despite wartime petrol rationing and vehicle shortages, and was followed within weeks by the Cheshire-based company Crosville which opened new cross-boundary routes from Crewe to Whitchurch and from Nantwich to Market Drayton. Crosville would go on to acquire Wrexham and District in 1934, resulting in Oswestry and the far north of Shropshire becoming their territory rather than that of Midland Red.

The first local bus services in the Shrewsbury area also began in 1915, opened with a single vehicle by the Allen Omnibus Company. On the 1st April 1916 the business was sold to Midland Red and would be used as the beach-head for a more serious invasion of the county by the regional super-power. By 1925 there were Midland Red services from Shrewsbury to most of the county's major towns and across the border into Wales, and yet a glance at the route map would have failed to reveal the true picture. In reality only the services to Market Drayton, Newport via Wellington, Bridgnorth, and Ludlow operated at a useful frequency on roads convincingly secured from competition by other operators. To the north of Shrewsbury BMMO's half-hearted schedules could offer little to entice passengers away from the more frequent (and cheaper) services of independents based in the Oswestry and Whitchurch areas, while in the rural terrain to the west and southwest of the county town the larger operator's vehicles were soon chased away by locally owned buses which the villagers clearly preferred. Almost all of Midland Red's services to the west of the main (north-south) A49 trunk road had been relinquished by 1935. Several important daily services from Shrewsbury became dominated by independents as a result including major routes to Oswestry, Whitchurch, Bishops Castle and to the Welsh side of the border.

In the south of the county, around Ludlow, vehicles of Midland Red were already providing main road services northwards to Shrewsbury and southwards to Hereford by 1925, but not much else. This poor showing was improved somewhat in the early 1930s by the introduction of a direct route from Ludlow to Birmingham via Cleobury Mortimer and Kidderminster, basically an extended version of the trailblazing service introduced by the Worcestershire Motor Transport company back in 1915. Departures from Ludlow to Kidderminster were hourly or better with four journeys each day continuing on to the big city. Most other operations, ranging from daily services to neighbouring towns to single market-day runs to a bewildering number of outlying villages, were left to local independents with lower overheads who were proud to be of service to their native communities regardless of the marginal revenues available. Nobody could ever have hoped to make a fortune from stage-carriage work in southern Shropshire, not even the proprietor of the Corvedale Motor Company which blossomed briefly between 1939 and 1953 as the most important of all the locally-owned operators.

The A5 trunk route leading eastwards from Shrewsbury, once a part of the Roman road known as Watling Street which ran from London to Chester and later a component of Thomas Telford's remarkable highway from London to Anglesey, might have been expected to be safer territory for Midland Red vehicles, with its surrounding landscape of small industrial villages guaranteeing an abundance of customers for public transport services. BMMO responded to this demand by providing an hourly service from Shrewsbury to Wellington and Newport, and connections every two hours from Shrewsbury to Birmingham (and later beyond) via Wellington and Wolverhampton, and from Wellington to both Bridgnorth and Kidderminster. The potential for local services in the Wellington area was largely ignored, leaving attractive opportunities for small (often single vehicle) independent operators in nearby villages such as Dawley, Donnington, Hadley, Oakengates, St Georges and Trench.

The Wellington area operators first attracted serious attention from Midland Red in the years immediately before the 1930 Road Traffic Act, occasioned no doubt by the thought that it would be cheaper to drive them off the road (metaphorically speaking) than to buy their businesses at a later date when fully licensed by the new Traffic Commissioners. A few of the independents fell by the wayside, but the majority allied themselves into the Shropshire Omnibus Association (SOA) and prepared to fight for their livelihoods. Some must have wondered if it was all worthwhile, with industry and mining badly affected by the Great Depression and passenger revenues already in serious decline. Midland Red, by all accounts, held a similarly pessimistic view of the prospects for these microscopic competitors, and believed that it would be able to pick them up in the near future for a song and a very small cheque, despite the newly printed licences.

The ink on those licences was only just dry when the government announced that the British army's main weapons storage facility was to be moved from the Woolwich Arsenal in London to a new Central Ordnance Depot (COD) in Donnington, Shropshire, comfortably far enough inland to eliminate any possibility of a surprise attack by enemy forces. A major army garrison was planned as part of the new military complex, and several well-known engineering and munitions companies moved into the area to be closer to their main source of income. Wellington and the villages to the east regained their prosperity and the region's independent bus operators were saved from penury. They would continue in their highly individualistic endeavours for another four decades, a swarm of colourful gadflies fluttering around a rather dreary old carthorse.

Their perseverance was smiled upon one more time by providence. As the British Empire disintegrated in the 1950s the COD at Donnington (and its garrison) diminished in importance and by the middle of the decade passenger revenues were once again in decline. Some of the Shropshire Omnibus Association's members decided to retire before things became even worse, selling out to other SOA operators. Then came another government announcement; the area to the east of Wellington had been chosen as the site for a new town, incorporating most of the villages and surrounding each one of them with large housing and industrial estates. The vastly enlarged

Besides an odd selection of second-hand vehicles, the war brought an influx of Bedford OWB utility buses. This Mulliner-bodied example, BUX 877, is seen in service with Arthur of Oswestry shortly before the company's sale to Vagg of Knockin Heath. (Chris Warn Collection)

The Duple version of the OWB utility bus was virtually indistinguishable from those produced by Mulliner, Roe, SMT, and other government contractors. CAW 400 was owned by Freeman of Munslow (as seen here) until that business's sale to Boulton of Cardington in 1959. It gave Boulton a further three years of service. (SNJ White via Peter Harden)

Worthen & District was originally the trading name of founder BD Bunce, but in 1945 the company was sold to Mid-Wales Motorways which maintained it as a separate unit until 1958. This Crossley SD42 with Burlingham bus bodywork, AEP 712, was transferred from the parent fleet to Worthen in 1951 but moved back to Wales in 1952. (Peter Harden Collection)

Oswestry on a winter Wednesday in the late 1950s. On the left is Daimler CWA6/Duple utility bus GHA 946, new to Midland Red (who modified its bodywork), briefly operated by Lloyd of Oswestry, and then (as seen here) in the ownership of Bryn Melyn of Llangollen. The Bedford OB/Duple Vista in the centre was operated by Hyde of Ellesmere and the SBG/Super Vega on the right by another Welsh operator, Fisher of Bronington. (B Mel Gough Collection)

community would later be given the name of Telford in honour of the famous engineer who had revolutionised domestic travel with his canal and road projects. Midland Red found themselves as a minor player in this major new conurbation. On the Wellington to Oakengates group of services, for example, the Monday to Friday daytime frequency of every ten minutes required the use of six vehicles. Four came from the independents (on a rota system) and two from Midland Red. The same routes on Saturday afternoon (the busiest time of the week) needed no less than 13 vehicles, of which 10 were provided by SOA members and only three by Midland Red. The county's newest town, soon to rival Shrewsbury in population, was not a place where a supposedly monopolistic area agreement operator could bully the locals.

# Crossing The Boundaries

Not all of the independent bus services in the county were provided by Shropshire-based companies. In Whitchurch the dominant independent, the locally headquartered Salopia Saloon Coaches, had acquired most of its route network from a Flintshire operator, Chesworth of Bronington. For those unfamiliar with the history of the area it should perhaps be explained that the part of Wales which would eventually become Flintshire had previously been incorporated into the English county of Cheshire as a punishment for Welsh resistance in the thirteenth century. Returned to its original national jurisdiction in Tudor times (some two hundred years later), it consisted of two separate parcels of land, a major part along the Dee estuary and Irish Sea coast, and a smaller portion which was entirely surrounded by Denbighshire, Cheshire and Shropshire. The village of Bronington was located in this enclave, a mile from the Shropshire border and just over two miles from the market town of Whitchurch. On routes into this detached rectangle of Welsh territory Salopia faced competition from another Bronington company, William Fisher and Son, with services straddling the Shropshire-Flintshire boundary. Fisher's routes also included market-day runs to Ellesmere and Oswestry, and in early 1965 the company became one of the participants in a new limited-stop service from Whitchurch to Oswestry which replaced a closed passenger railway line. The other partners in this operation were Salopia, Hyde of Ellesmere, Hampson of

Oswestry and Crosville, and although the service ran at fairly infrequent intervals (and, being divided among five operators, was hardly a great money-spinner) it seemed to give the Fishers an appetite for further expansion into Shropshire. In 1966 they acquired a part of the business of Thomas Hyde & Son, including its Ellesmere garage, a pair of Bedfords and a minibus, and two market-day routes, one of which was wholly within Shropshire. The acquisition of Reeve of Ellesmere in 1968 (a one-vehicle operator with a Tuesday market service) and the more substantial M & G Motors of Wem in 1974 would further extend the Welsh operator's English operations.

Oswestry attracted Welsh operators from a westerly direction as well as Fisher's services from the east. Denbighshire independents included Hughes Brothers of Llansilin (with a weekday service from the villages beyond Offa's Dyke), LG Phillips of Glynceiriog (trading as Ceiriog Valley Transport) who came in from Llanarmon on a weekday service jointly operated with Vagg, and Bryn Melyn Motor Services of Llangollen which ran a Wednesday-only route to Oswestry from its home town. Bryn Melyn sometimes used double-deckers on this service, which demonstrated its popularity among Welsh shoppers. One independent operator from Montgomeryshire, Tom Davies of Llanfihangel, also ran into Oswestry on market days, his aging Bedford OB packed to the gills with residents from tiny villages around the shores of Lake Vyrnwy.

A more substantial invader from Montgomeryshire could be found in Shrewsbury where Mid-Wales Motorways of Newtown was one of the leading independent operators. Mid-Wales provided a daily service into the Shropshire county town from Welshpool along with a weekday route from Four Crosses and Crewe Green. The company's fleet was never less than amazing, and until 1967 included a variety of second-hand double-deckers as well as a glorious mixture of saloons ranging from the de rigueur Bedford OBs expected of rural operators to Commer Avenger buses with Saro and Strachan bodywork, Sentinels, a quintet of archaic Dennis Lancet buses acquired from Merthyr Tydfil Corporation and the Yeates Pegasus previously mentioned which crammed 53 passengers into its 31 feet of bodywork (the Pegasus design more usually seated a maximum of 45). A separate book could easily be written on the subject of Mid-Wales Motorways alone, and I intend to give the company greater attention in a future volume covering the independents of North Wales.

In the south of Shropshire the intruders were of English origin. Griffiths of Leintwardine in Herefordshire (trading as Teme Valley) provided tri-county links from Knighton in Radnorshire to Ludlow and Craven Arms in Shropshire, both services running via its home village. Until 1954 these routes had been operated by the Yeomans family's various enterprises, passing first to the Corvedale Motor Company and then to Griffiths in 1960. The Ludlow service was daily, albeit infrequent, while the route to Craven Arms ran on three days per week.

Further east the small Worcestershire market town of Tenbury Wells was situated on the southern bank of the River Teme, a literal stone's throw from the Shropshire village of Burford across the river. As might be expected it attracted independents from both counties. Corvedale operated a daily service from Ludlow, while another daily service from the Shropshire village of Hopton Bank had been pioneered by the Cleobury Mortimer independent Charles Motor Services. In January 1952 the Charles business was acquired by M & M Coaches of Kidderminster in Worcestershire which kept the Shropshire garage and continued to operate the Tenbury Wells route under the M & M name along with several less frequent market-day runs to other surrounding towns. From the south another Worcestershire company, Yarranton Brothers of Eardiston, left its 'comfort zone' by offering a market-day only service which crossed the river into Shropshire before turning eastwards back into its home county.

The area close to the Staffordshire boundary was dominated by the market town of Newport, a Shropshire community where most of the independently run bus services were provided by a Staffordshire company, GH Austin and Son of Woodseaves. Austin's home village was only a few miles away from Newport which explained the anomaly. Besides its trunk route from Stafford to Newport (with some journeys continuing to Donnington and Hadley) the company also acquired market-day runs to numerous villages in eastern Shropshire, and one of these extended to reach Wellington on Thursdays. In 1964 Austin's vehicles began to appear in Wellington on a more

regular basis when the company was awarded a daily rail-replacement service from Stafford and Newport. This proved to be a mixed blessing, as the Stafford to Newport half of the route diverted passengers from its own existing 'stopping' services, while the Newport to Wellington end suffered from severe traffic restrictions. As a result of these difficulties Austin withdrew the service when the railway subsidy expired. The Thursday-only run from Newport to Wellington would be withdrawn shortly thereafter as part of the more general cutbacks associated with Austin's financial meltdown.

For the purposes of this book a Shropshire independent is defined as one with its headquarters and principal garage within the county, so neither Fisher of Bronington nor M & M of Kidderminster are included although I intend to cover both operators in future volumes. Those with an appetite for more information on Austins (the bus company, not the car manufacturer!) are referred to my previous volume on Staffordshire independents published by Venture in April 2009. Readers should also note the omission of Griffiths of Leintwardine, definitely a Herefordshire operator despite some confusion caused by the Post Office which delivered the village's mail 'via Ludlow' in Shropshire. For more pragmatic reasons (the enormous number of individuals and companies which have contributed to the local bus industry over the years, many of them leaving few traces) operators which ceased to exist before 1960 are also omitted from the main text, although most of those which survived into the 1950s are mentioned in passing along with brief details of the ultimate disposal of their services. As is generally the case with books in the Venture Prestige/Super Prestige series the coverage ends with deregulation, leaving others at a later date to tell the more recent history of the subject. These parameters may seem artificially restrictive, but the period between the 1950s and 1986 is undoubtedly an era worthy of study, particularly as it coincides with the years for which most (older) enthusiasts feel an acute, almost painful, sense of nostalgia. Younger readers are invited aboard too, to explore an age when British buses were built by an enormous variety of British manufacturers and run by companies controlled by their colourful founders rather than by colourless accountants and clueless university graduates. It was a different age and in many ways preferable to the present.

Yet another foreigner, but this time in Shrewsbury's famous Barker Street bus station. Extremely rare Commer Avenger I/Saunders bus OUA 76 of Mid-Wales Motorways is parked in front of its MWM 'duplicate', Sentinel STC4/40 CEP 147. To the left is Avenger I/Churchill coach CEP 264, once with MWM but by the time of this photograph in service with TJ Green's Worthen Motorways operation. (Martin Bayley Collection)

There were also trespassers across the county's southern boundaries. In January 1952 M & M Coaches of Kidderminster (in Worcestershire) acquired Charles Motor Services of Cleobury Mortimer along with 12 vehicles and several rural stage services. M & M's new routes were usually operated by coaches, but in May 1963 the company acquired this 1947 PS1 Tiger/Burlingham bus, HG 9512, from Burnley Colne & Nelson to cover the Cleobury services. It was sold to a Welsh operator in September 1964. (Chris Warn Collection)

# Acknowledgments

This is an unashamedly nostalgic book, and in any such volume the photographic content is easily as important as the written word. Approximately one-third of the photographs presented here (including the vast majority of those which illustrate the 'Wellington and Telford' chapter) are drawn from the collection of vehicle preservationist B Mel Gough who was kind enough to give me access to his impressive archive. Without his assistance the book would have been much less comprehensive. Many of the photographs in Mel's collection were originally taken by one of the 20th century's most famous bus and coach photographers, Roy Marshall, who did us all an enormous service by pointing his camera at vehicles neglected by others – particularly in the county of Shropshire. Roy has now retired from his tireless travels around the nation and I fear that we may never see his equal again.

Several other individuals made generous and labour-intensive searches of their photographic collections to help complete this project. Notable among their number are vehicle preservationist Chris Elmes (who owns several coaches previously operated by Shropshire independents) Peter Harden (now living in Northern Ireland but still in possession of an impressive 'mainland' collection from days gone by), Geoff Mills (best known for his sterling work in recording the history of East Anglian independents), and Malcolm Yeomans (who has migrated to France but still drives for Boultons during his visits to Britain). Once again, Roy Marshall's superb photographs feature prominently in the collections of most of these contributors (as do other famous names such as JF Higham. Robert F Mack and SNJ White) and are credited accordingly. Several other illustrations came from the collections of Martin Bayley, Tim Butler, Malcolm Knight, Philip Mountford and Eric Wain and all are thanked for their valuable contributions. As usual photographs of unknown provenance are credited to the collections of those who submitted them and profuse apologies are offered to any photographers whose original work remains unacknowledged.

Many of these gentlemen also assisted with historical material, as did John Howie, Peter Johnson, David Miller and Trevor Williams. As is ever the case, the reference works published by the Omnibus Society and the PSV Circle have proven to be invaluable in the preparation of this book, and cannot be recommended too highly. Several prominent members of the Omnibus Society have been particularly helpful in providing information to the author, including Alan W Mills (who also volunteered to check the manuscript for errors, although any that remain are entirely my own!) and Chris Warn (who gave me access to his unbelievably comprehensive archive covering PSV activity in Shropshire from the pioneering days to the present). The Omnibus Society's Photographic Registrar, Alan Oxley, also contributed to the finished product by searching for some rare Roy Marshall negatives unavailable elsewhere.

My continuing computer illiteracy has made the contributions of several other individuals essential to the completion of the book. Among them are my daughter Helena Mercer (who knew more about computers by the age of 14 than I will ever learn) and my good friends Samantha Hardy and Philip Cryer. The three of them are still trying to drag me, kicking and screaming, into the 21st century. Finally, my thanks go to my editor, Bob Rowe, and to all at Venture Publications for their support and for offering me the chance to bring this story to a wider audience. Your work behind the scenes is appreciated more than you will ever know, by authors and readers alike!

Neville Mercer
January 2011

Somewhat surprisingly, the ubiquitous ex-London Transport RT double-decker was entirely absent from the fleets of Shropshire's independent stage-carriage operators. There were, however, some ex-London STLs, RFs, and GSs to be found. This is Lloyd of Oswestry's STL type AYV 612. Note the profusion of traffic notices in the windows, most of which would have been advertising excursions and the company's express service to Blackpool. (Peter Harden Collection)

A typical Corvedale driver, attired in cloth cap and tie, awaits departure time in the entrance of Guy Vixen/ECW 26-seater MXX 372. New to London Transport in 1953 as GS72, the vehicle was one of a pair of early disposals which arrived in Ludlow in March 1963. When photographed here it was still in LT Country Area livery, but will be portrayed in Corvedale colours on a later page. (Author's Collection)

Bartley of Selattyn acquired this 1947 Harrington bodied Commer Commando, BJG 834, from Sayers of Margate in July 1956. It remained in service until 1962. The vehicle just visible behind it is Bartley's OB/Vista LAF 407 and both are in variations of the operator's green and cream livery. (Roy Marshall via the Omnibus Society)

And here is a better view of LAF 407, a 1948 OB which Bartley acquired in July 1953. The Cornish registration (it had been new to the famous Penryn & Falmouth Motor Co) was unusual in Shropshire and might find a ready buyer today among comedians with a taste for cherished number-plates. Bartley replaced the vehicle with an SB/Vega in 1965. (Roy Marshall)

# Part One
# OSWESTRY AND THE NORTH

The northern end of the county of Shropshire has much in common with the neighbouring county of Cheshire. Geographically speaking, the countryside is essentially flat with few noticeable hills and no major rivers suitable for boats beyond the size of a modest canoe. The local economy remains largely dependent upon agriculture, in both its arable and dairy-farming variants, although in days gone by the extraction of peat for use as a domestic fuel was also an important source of income. The principal retail centres are still to be found in the traditional market towns of Oswestry, Whitchurch and Market Drayton (with more limited shopping opportunities available in Ellesmere and Wem), while those in search of brighter lights must travel northwards to Chester or southwards to Shrewsbury.

Peat would be replaced by another natural resource. By the middle of the 18th century the Industrial Revolution had begun in the Severn Valley, and the ironmasters of Coalbrookdale had developed a considerable appetite for coal to feed their furnaces. In the north-west of the county, on the Denbighshire border, several major 'pits' were developed to meet this new demand and the great age of canal-building began, made necessary by the inadequacy of the inland road network which had deteriorated relentlessly since Roman times. In northern Shropshire the coalfield immediately to the north of Oswestry was served by the Llangollen Canal (which also passed close to Ellesmere and Whitchurch), while Market Drayton became a boom-town thanks to the proximity of the Shropshire Union Canal which connected the Mersey Estuary to the West Midlands. An even greater revolution in the transportation industry began in the 1830s when the first practical railway lines were built. One of the earliest 'cross-country' routes ran from Crewe to Shrewsbury, Hereford and South Wales, passing through the northern Shropshire towns of Whitchurch and Wem and further increasing their economic growth as a result. Within a century the county of Shropshire would have more railway stations than anywhere else in the country, and

although most of them were insignificant rural 'halts' they still allowed access to national markets for a host of local products ranging from coal and milk to the whalebone corsets manufactured in the Whitchurch and Market Drayton workshops of the famous 'Silhouette' company.

The Second World War brought another economic boom to northern Shropshire as the Royal Air Force found the level countryside ideal for its purposes and built a large number of aerodromes in the region. Major facilities were quickly commissioned at Shawbury, Ternhill, High Ercall, Sleap and Tilstock, resulting in a density of available runways unrivalled outside of the equally flat terrain of East Anglia and Lincolnshire on the opposite side of the country. Shawbury has remained as a major RAF base into the 21st century (latterly as a helicopter training school), while Ternhill has survived as a gliding site for RAF cadets, and both Sleap and Tilstock have seen further use by civilian aviators since their 'demobilisation' by the military.

As early beneficiaries of developments in the canal and railway industries, it was perhaps to be expected that the people of northern Shropshire would embrace the new motor-bus with equally open arms. Ellis Chesworth's pioneering network of routes around Whitchurch has already been mentioned in the introduction and many were to follow his lead, providing the region with a comprehensive web of independent bus services which was little short of a marvel to behold in such a fundamentally rural area.

## Bartley of Selattyn

The village of Selattyn is on the road from Oswestry to Glynceiriog, less than a mile to the east of Offa's Dyke, and has always been poorly served by the public transport network. For almost seventy years the community's only bus services were market-day only runs to Oswestry provided by members of the Bartley family.

By November 1930 Mr JR Bartley was operating a 14-seat Chevrolet LQ bus on these services and in 1931 received licences for the Glynceiriog-Selattyn-Oswestry and Selattyn-Wern-Oswestry routes along with excursions and tours from the local area. In April 1934 the Chevrolet was replaced by a 20-seat Commer Centaur and in 1941 a second-hand Bedford WTB coach arrived from Arthur of Oswestry. A new

Bedford OB/Duple Vista coach was delivered in March 1949 and was followed by two second-hand examples in 1952/53. Variety was provided by a Harrington bodied Commer Commando coach which arrived in July 1956 and replaced one of the second-hand OBs.

The founder died in 1958 and control of the business passed to his widow, Mrs Winifred Bartley. In February 1961 she acquired the company's first Bedford SB and over the next decade further examples of this type would replace the remaining OBs and the Commando. Little else changed until late 1973 when Mrs Bartley died and left the business to her children, JR Bartley Jr (who served as the conductor on the stage services) and Mrs Doris Morris (who performed some of the driving duties). At around the same time the first SB (by then more than 20 years old) was replaced by a brand-new 29-seat Bedford VAS with Duple Bella Vista bodywork.

Deregulation was very much a non-event in Selattyn with nobody else particularly interested in competing with Bartley's services. Declining traffic did however take its toll, and in December 1992 the Glynceiriog-Selattyn-Oswestry service (by then numbered 411) became Wednesday only

after the withdrawal of the Saturday timings. The end finally came in July 1999 when the proprietors decided to retire and the remaining journeys were allocated to other operators.

# Butter of Childs Ercall

In 1927 Charles Hamilton Butter acquired an eight-seat Chevrolet taxi and began to offer a weekday service from the village of Childs Ercall to the nearby town of Market Drayton. The first 'real' bus, a second-hand 14-seat Chevrolet, arrived in April 1930 and was followed by a brand-new 20-seat Bedford WLB in August 1931. The new Traffic Commissioners awarded Butter licences for the Market Drayton route and for another (daily except Wednesdays) service from Hatton and Childs Ercall to Wellington. Business continued to boom and in 1935 Butter acquired a five year old 32-seat Guy Conquest from Birmingham Corporation. This vehicle obviously impressed as many more Guys would follow it into the fleet.

In January 1939 another 32-seater arrived in the shape of a second-hand Maudslay, and in May 1940 Butter acquired the Market Drayton to Stoke Heath service of Evans along with a Bedford WLB. This service passed RAF Ternhill (as did Butter's

DCK 111 (seen here running on Guy Motors' trade-plates 039 UK because we could not find a view in service) was an Arab III which carried the prototype of Lincolnshire Trailers' "Crellin-Duplex" half-decker design. Seating 46 passengers (HDC22/24F) it was delivered new to Fargher of Walmer Bridge near Preston (trading as "Ambler Pullman") in 1950. Butter bought it in January 1953, but it frightened customers away and was sold to the Don Everall dealership in early 1954. (Author's Collection/Guy Motors)

In 1947-49 Butter of Childs Ercall bought seven new Guy Arab III coaches and four Guy Vixen buses from a dealer in Hanley, hence the Stoke-on-Trent registration of 1948's Barnard-bodied Arab III MEH 191. The vehicle was sold in 1959 and appears to have vanished, probably into the arms of an eager scrap dealer. (Author's Collection)

A further two Vixen buses delivered in 1949 had Shropshire registrations. This is the first of the pair (also bodied by Barnard), FAW 725. It was withdrawn from use in 1961. The location is Butter's rural base, and visible in the garage behind is the rear end of identical vehicle MVT 86 which was withdrawn in 1960. Note the differing colour schemes although both are blue and cream. (Author's Collection)

As the registration suggests this PS1 Tiger/Roe bodied bus, AHE 776, had been new to Yorkshire Traction in 1947. Butter acquired it from Holt of Manchester in September 1959 and sold it for scrap six years later. (B Mel Gough Collection)

AEC-Beadle rebuild NKT 933 was assembled, Frankenstein fashion, for Maidstone & District in 1951 using pre-war running units. It arrived with Butter from Sportsman of Whiston (near St Helens, Lancashire) in June 1960. Withdrawn from service in June 1965, a visitor noticed it in derelict condition at the garage two years later and it was presumably scrapped. (Author's Collection)

Butter also bought three second-hand Guy Vixens between 1954 and 1960. This is the third to arrive, LTC 164, and unusual in carrying Longwell Green bodywork. Another vehicle from a St Helens operator (Stubbs), it was presumably purchased from the same dealer as the AEC-Beadle and possibly on the same day out! Built in 1949 it became Butter's last Vixen and remained in service until 1964. (Author's Collection)

Second-hand Bedford SBs were another common sight on Butter's services in the 1960s. Burlingham bodied YEH 913 (new in 1956) arrived at Childs Ercall from its original owner, Stonier of Goldenhill, in May 1963 and lasted into the early 1970s. (Author's Collection)

original route) and much of the company's wartime activity involved the provision of services to the aerodromes at Ternhill, Shawbury and High Ercall. This work brought a profusion of second-hand buses and coaches to Childs Ercall (including vehicles of AJS, Bedford, Chevrolet, Commer, Guy, Leyland, Opel, Reo and Vulcan manufacture) along with five government-allocated Bedford OWB utility buses. Many of the second-hand vehicles were ready for the scrapyard by the end of the war and all had gone by the summer of 1948, replaced by six new Guy Arab III coaches, three new Bedford OBs (two coaches, one of them with unusual Auto-Cellulose bodywork, and a Duple-bodied bus), and a Burlingham-bodied Crossley SD42 bus.

During the war Butter had started a new local circular service in Market Drayton, serving the RAF Married Quarters at Buntingsdale Hall. This continued into peace-time along with a Saturday-only route from Hinstock (site of another RAF facility) to Shrewsbury via Hatton and Childs Ercall. Further work was provided for the new vehicles by a network of 'Forces Leave' express services radiating from RAF Shawbury to Birkenhead (for Liverpool), Birmingham, Crewe Railway Station, Derby and Stoke-on-Trent.

In 1949 the wartime OWBs were replaced by a fleet of six brand-new 29-seat Guy Vixen buses, five bodied by Barnard of Norwich, the other by Ormac of Preston. The gradual rundown of the RAF presence in the Market Drayton area in the early 1950s brought a change in vehicle buying policy and most subsequent vehicles would be purchased from other operators via dealers. These included machines of AEC, Albion, Beadle, Bedford, Commer, Daimler, Dennis, Ford, Guy, Leyland, Seddon, Tilling-Stevens and Vulcan manufacture, making the small village of Childs Ercall a Utopia for visiting bus enthusiasts. The solitary Daimler (a CWA6 which came from Yeomans of Canon Pyon via Don Everall) was also the only double-decker ever operated by Butter, while the Guys included three second-hand Vixens, the famously ugly Arab III/Lincolnshire Trailer 'half-decker' prototype DCK 111, and the Arab UF demonstrator GUY 3.

The founder passed away in July 1966 and was succeeded by a partnership of his widow, his daughter and his son Stanley who became the new de facto proprietor. RAF-related traffic continued to dwindle and by 1971 the fleet had shrunk from its peak of more than 20 to just seven vehicles. The stage-carriage services were also being adversely affected by car ownership and Stanley Butter compensated for these factors by bidding aggressively for schools contracts and private-hire work. At deregulation in 1986/87 the rural bus routes were lost to other operators but the Market Drayton town services continued until 2005 when they too were lost to lower bidders. A limited company, Butters Coaches, had replaced the private partnership in 2003 and this entity concentrated on the schools, excursions and private-hire sectors until its unexpected closure in July 2009. It was a tragic ending for such a colourful operator.

## Gittins of Crickheath

In 1921 the brothers Dan and Jack Gittins established the Service Garage in Crickheath, a small village on a minor road to the south of Oswestry. They bought a Ford Model T lorry-bus in 1922 and in August of that year began a market-day only service to Oswestry via three different routes. A second Ford arrived in 1925 and the pair were replaced in 1928/30 by two purpose-built Vulcan buses. These continued the Crickheath services and opened a new market-day route from Sweeney Mountain to Oswestry. The Gittins brothers were also awarded excursions and tours licences from both Crickheath and Oswestry by the new Traffic Commissioners.

After the Vulcans all subsequent vehicles were of either Bedford or Leyland manufacture, the former including a pre-war Wilmott-bodied WTB bus and two post-war OB/Duple Vista coaches, and the latter a 1935 Burlingham-bodied Cub replaced in turn by a 1948 Burlingham-bodied Tiger half-cab and then a late-model 1954 Royal Tiger with Burlingham Seagull bodywork. Besides the Wednesday/Saturday services to Oswestry, the excursions and tours, and private-hire work, the Gittins also acquired an attractive schools service which ran from Pant Crossroads to Moreton School via Llynclys. Content to remain a very small business, with the two brothers undertaking most of the driving and maintenance, the fleet stabilised at three vehicles in the post-war era. Of eleven buses and coaches acquired between 1922 and 1966 all but one were new, the exception being a Duple-bodied Bedford SB3 coach bought from Salopia in 1963 to replace the older of the two OBs.

Not the best of photographs, but the subject matter makes it irresistible. This is the Gittins brothers' 14-seat Vulcan UX 6439, new to them in 1930. The vehicle lasted for ten years at Crickheath. (Roy Marshall Collection via the Omnibus Society)

The Bedford OB with Duple Vista bodywork is surely one of the five most important designs in the history of the industry. This immaculate 1950 example is GUJ 356 in service with its original owners, Gittins of Crickheath. Their stylish 'winged letter G' emblem is just visible in front of the rear wheel arch. When Dan and Jack retired the vehicle passed to Mid-Wales Motorways and survives in preservation. (Author's Collection)

Inevitably, retirement soon loomed for the Gittins brothers and in December 1966 they sold the goodwill of the business (including its route licences) to Parish of Morda (qv). The vehicles were sold separately with the surviving OB going to Mid-Wales Motorways (which still had an appetite for such things), the Royal Tiger/Seagull to Vagg of Knockin Heath and the second-hand SB3 to a dealer who later exported it to Ireland. Three of the eleven vehicles owned by Gittins (the 1948 Tiger, the final OB and the Seagull) survive in preservation although at present all carry the liveries of later operators. Suitably repainted in brown and cream they could provide the nucleus for a magnificent 'Oswestry Running Day' at some point in the future, perhaps in 2012 to celebrate the 90th anniversary of Gittins' first bus services. Let's do it!

# Hampson of Oswestry

James Hampson went into business in 1921 with a Chevrolet char-a-banc, bought a second one in 1923 and a third in 1925. The first bus came in June 1929 with the purchase of a 14-seat Chevrolet LQ, bought for a new daily stage-carriage service from Oswestry to Whittington and Babbinswood, expanding villages close to the main Ellesmere road. In 1931 this service was licensed by the new Traffic Commissioners along with excursions and tours from the Oswestry area. The Chevrolet brand was merged into the new Bedford marque from 1931 and Hampson remained loyal to the manufacturer, buying six more before the start of the Second World War although no more than four were in the fleet at the same time.

Curiously (given the presence of the large Park Hall army camp on the outskirts of Oswestry), Hampson received no allocation of either new or second-hand vehicles during the war, and three of the pre-war WTBs soldiered on until the late 1940s when they were replaced by four Bedford OBs. These included a 'standard' Duple Vista coach, two fully-fronted coaches bodied by Plaxton and a 31-seat Mulliner bodied bus. Another vehicle purchased new in 1948, a Yeates bodied Dennis Lancet coach, proved more short-lived and was replaced in the following year by two Crossleys with Bellhouse Hartwell bodywork.

The founder's son, Douglas, became a partner in 1947 and by the summer of 1956 the Hampsons were operating five OBs (three coaches and two buses), the two Crossley coaches, a new Bedford SBG/Duple Super Vega coach, and a Willowbrook bodied Daimler CVD6 bus, the latter recently acquired from Shotters of the Isle of Wight. The growth of the business had been driven by new housing along the Ellesmere road and (from 1953) by new 'Forces Leave' express services from Park Hall camp to Birkenhead, Birmingham, London and Manchester. In 1957 Hampson introduced a new 'Town' service in Oswestry, a weekday operation which had the peculiarity of ending at lunchtime on Thursday which was the community's 'early closing day'. New arrivals in the late 1950s were three more second-hand OBs (including a Beadle bodied bus from Hants & Dorset), two additional Bedford SBs (which replaced the Crossleys) and a Foden PVSC6 coach acquired from a Cheshire operator.

The Foden was a break with tradition (being the first Gardner engined vehicle in the fleet), but its peculiarity was swiftly overshadowed in March 1960 by the arrival of two Albion Nimbuses with 29-seat dual-purpose bodywork by Alexander. The vehicles came from the coach operator Jackson of Castle Bromwich which had acquired them new (along with a third identical machine) in 1957. Intended for use on the 'Town' service (which negotiated some narrow streets and tight corners) they rapidly proved themselves unsuitable for this work due to poor reliability and were reallocated to excursion and private-hire duties. In 1962 they were replaced by a second 1946-vintage Beadle-bodied OB bus and a 1955 Bedford SB with Duple Midland bodywork.

In the spring of 1961 another Oswestry operator, JW Lloyd and Sons, decided to give up its interests in the bus and coach industry. Hampson bought their Oswestry to Babbinswood service (which competed with their own along most of its route), a seasonal express service from Oswestry to Blackpool and two early-model Bedford SB coaches. The remainder of the Lloyd business passed to Crosville later in the same year. As a result of this expansion it was decided to form a limited company and this materialised as Hampsons Luxury Coaches Ltd in 1963. For unknown reasons the registered office of this company was located at Newton Abbot in Devon.

The military express services from Park Hall came to an end in 1962 but in 1964 were partially replaced by new 'shoppers' express services

Many bodybuilders had problems with adapting their designs to suit the radiator cowlings of Foden vehicles, even Burlingham who made a good job of most things. This is PVSC6 coach AHF 785, new to Cox of Wallasey in 1950 and acquired by Hampson of Oswestry in January 1959. In July 1963 it was resold to a Herefordshire operator. (Peter Harden Collection)

When Hampson started its Oswestry 'Town' service in 1957 it needed to expand its service bus fleet. This Bedford OB with unattractive bus bodywork by Beadle, JEL 277, was new to Hants & Dorset in 1949. Nine years later it came to Oswestry and acquired cove panel advertising for a local ironmonger. It went to a firm of contractors in August 1967. (Author's Collection)

Mulliner's Bedford OB bus design was much easier on the eye than Beadle's. Hampson bought this 1948 vehicle, EUJ 855, in May 1960 but kept it for less than two years before selling it to Wellington Grammar School in April 1962. (Peter Harden Collection)

The Denbighshire registration indicates that this Bedford SBG/Duple Midland bus, MUN 91, was an import from Wales. New to Johnson of Southsea (the one near Wrexham) in 1955, it was sold to Hampson in April 1962 and directly replaced the OB/Mulliner pictured above. It passed to a dealer in March 1966 and saw further service elsewhere. (Author's Collection)

Hampson's brace of second-hand Albion Nimbuses with Alexander dual-purpose bodywork were bought with the 'Town' service in mind but proved too unreliable and ended up on coaching duties. UOF 600 is seen in Blackpool on the express service acquired from Lloyd in 1961. New to Jackson of Castle Bromwich in 1957, the two vehicles served with Hampson from 1960 until 1963. (Peter Harden Collection)

The long-term replacement for the aging OBs on the 'Town' service were a pair of 'private hire RF type' AEC Regal IVs acquired from London Transport in January 1964. They remained in service until the early 1980s, having given 17 years of their lives to Hampson compared to only 13 with London Transport. (Peter Harden Collection)

from Oswestry to Manchester (on Tuesdays) and Liverpool (on Thursdays). Another interesting development in 1964 was the purchase of two short wheelbase 'private-hire RF' AEC Regal IVs from London Transport. These 35-seat buses replaced the surviving Bedford OBs on the 'Town' service and also ventured out to Whittington and Babbinswood as back-up vehicles to the SB bus which remained as the principal vehicle on these more rural routes. The two RFs would remain in the Hampson fleet until 1981, giving the Oswestry company 17 years of service compared to only 13 spent with London Transport.

From the beginning of 1965 the RFs were also regular performers on a new rail-replacement service from Oswestry to Ellesmere and Whitchurch jointly operated by Hampson, Fisher of Bronington, Hyde of Ellesmere, Salopia of Whitchurch, and Crosville (which referred to it as the D87). A further presence along this road came in July 1966 when Hyde of Ellesmere (qv) sold its services into Oswestry from Ellesmere and Lower Frankton to Hampson along with an OB bus and an SB coach. Both of the vehicles had been resold by the end of the year.

For almost 15 years all of Hampson's purchases were of either Bedford or AEC manufacture until two 45-seat Bristol LH buses were acquired from Trent Motor Traction to replace the long-serving RFs. More drastic changes were afoot. In early 1980 the Hampson family sold the company to the TE Jones Group of Nesscliffe, a plant-hire firm which had owned Vagg of Knockin Heath (qv) since 1974. At first the Hampson business remained a separate entity, but in April 1982 its services and assets were merged with those of Vagg under the latter's name. An unexpected resurrection came before the end of the year. In September 1982 the TE Jones Group went into liquidation, taking its subsidiaries with it. Vagg would disappear forever as a result, but negotiations had already been underway to 'hive off' the former Hampson assets as a means of saving the entire group. The receivers continued with this potential deal and sold the Hampson brand-name, the goodwill of the route licences, and most of the former Hampson vehicles to Robert C Lunt.

Mr Lunt, who had less than a year's experience as a private-hire operator, re-launched the company as 'Hampson 82' but soon found himself competing with Owens Coaches which received identical licences under the newly liberalised regulations. Neither operator made much money and in June 1987 Mr Lunt's company (Gela Ltd) went into liquidation, bringing the Hampson story to an end.

# Hyde of Ellesmere

In 1921 Thomas Hyde, a resident of the small village of Welsh Frankton between Ellesmere and Whitchurch, bought a Ford Model T and began to offer the vehicle for hire. Initially, most of the work involved farm produce and livestock being transported to Ellesmere and Oswestry for sale, but the Ford could also be fitted with primitive bench seating and was soon operating passenger excursions on local market-days. Demand for these outings escalated and in 1925 Hyde bought a second Model T equipped as a 14-seat bus and began timetabled services from Ellesmere, Tetchill and the Franktons to Oswestry on Wednesdays and Saturdays.

A 14-seat Fiat was purchased in 1928 but was replaced three years later by the first of many Bedfords, a 20-seat WHB. A similar WLB followed in 1932, and in 1935 the fleet grew to three vehicles with the acquisition of a 1928 vintage 20-seat Vulcan from Gittins of Crickheath. Two new Bedford WTBs (a 25-seat bus and a 26-seat coach) arrived in the latter half of the 1930s and replaced the two smaller Bedfords. Another of the breed, a 32-seat OWB utility bus, replaced the Vulcan in 1943 and was the only wartime delivery.

After the war the company, by then known as Thomas Hyde and Son to reflect the inclusion of the founder's son and heir Thomas Harry Hyde, acquired new premises in Ellesmere to allow for a modest expansion in the size of the fleet. Deliveries in 1946 were of a brand-new Bedford OB coach and a second-hand WTB to join the two examples already operated. Three years later an influx of new vehicles (a Guy Vixen, an Austin CXB, and a second OB) replaced two of the pre-war WTBs, while in 1951 the third was supplanted by a 33-seat Bedford SB with Duple Vega bodywork. Another 1951 delivery was a 30-seat OB bus which subsequently operated most of the stage-carriage services and allowed the wartime OWB to be sold in 1953. It was replaced by another (third-hand) Austin CXB coach.

Later deliveries were of a second SB/Duple coach (new in 1958), an ex-Crosville OB/Duple coach (acquired in 1959 along with a new 11-seat Austin minibus), another OB with comparatively rare Strachan coach bodywork (purchased from a dealer in 1960 and sold two years later) and a 12-seat Commer minibus (which replaced the 1959 Austin version in 1963). Some welcome extra work came to the company in early 1965 when it became a participant in the rail-replacement service from Whitchurch to Ellesmere and Oswestry.

In July 1966 Mr Hyde Jr decided to retire and sold the business's assets to two neighbouring operators. Fisher of Bronington acquired the Ellesmere garage (which later passed to Lakeside Coaches), the 1951 SB, the ex-Crosville OB and the Commer minibus along with market-day routes from Tetchill to Oswestry and Ellesmere, while Hampson of Oswestry (qv) received the 1951 OB bus, the 1958 SB coach and the daily services between Ellesmere and Oswestry.

# Jones of Market Drayton

In 1926 Mr Vernon H Jones began regular services from his home village of Crickmerry to Market Drayton, trading as Wistanswick Bus Service. Less frequent operations soon linked the town to villages in the Woore area. The original vehicles remain unknown, but by 1931 a Ford Model AA and a Bedford WHB were in service. Two 20-seat WLBs were acquired in 1935/36 (one new, the other from Arthur of Oswestry), and at around the same time the operational base was moved to Market Drayton and the new trading name of VH Jones & Co was adopted. The first three actual coaches to be acquired (previous vehicles had bus seating) were an Albion (bought new in 1936), a Bedford WTB (new in 1938) and a year-old Maudslay (also bought in 1938).

Jones' main weekday service to Market Drayton ran via Ternhill, where a major RAF aerodrome was built in the late 1930s. This development kept traffic buoyant and led to two OWB utility buses being allocated to the operator in 1943. In addition to the route which passed Ternhill, Jones also began contract services between Market Drayton and RAF Shawbury. Post-war bus deliveries were few and far between and usually involved new and second-hand Bedford OBs, but there were a few exceptions including a Burlingham-bodied Crossley operated from 1948 to 1950 and a Duple Midland-bodied SB3, new

in 1959 and sold in 1964. The coaching side of the business, in contrast, expanded rapidly after the war with no fewer than 24 new vehicles being delivered between 1947 and 1951, most having a comparatively short stay before being replaced by newer specimens. The coaches acquired during this period were of Bedford, Crossley, Dennis, Leyland and Maudslay manufacture.

From 1953 to 1956 the company (known as Jones Coachways Ltd since 1947) changed its policy and acquired nine second-hand Bedford SB coaches alongside seven similar machines bought new. A trio of Commer Avenger IVs arrived in 1957 but were soon discarded and replaced by still more new Bedfords. No full-size buses were purchased after the 1959 SB3 and from 1964 onwards the stage services were maintained by vehicles with coach seating as were several new works services which connected the Market Drayton region with factories in Telford New Town.

After deregulation in 1986 Jones became the successful bidder for a number of services well outside of its traditional catchment area and these were usually operated by Mercedes-Benz minicoaches. This work continued well into the 1990s, but by November 1996 an increase in competition in the local coaching arena had driven Jones Coachways into the hands of the bankruptcy court.

# Lloyd of Oswestry

In 1920 Wrexham & District opened a single vehicle out-station in Oswestry. The regular driver of the Oswestry-based machine was Mr John W Lloyd, who soon branched out by acquiring a 12-seat Wolseley and offering excursions and private-hires. A small Fiat char-a-banc followed and in 1923 Mr Lloyd decided to eliminate any possible conflict of interest with his employers by leaving to establish his own bus company.

His first service bus, a 14-seat Ford Model T, arrived shortly afterwards and inaugurated two daily services. One ran northwards to Chirk and Black Park in direct competition with Wrexham & District, the other was a local service from Oswestry to the town's racecourse. Vehicle deliveries between 1923 and the start of the Second World War included a Vulcan char-a-banc (in 1924), an 18-seat Dennis coach (in 1929), two Chevrolets (in 1930), a second-hand Tilling-Stevens (in 1932) and a pair of Bedfords (in 1934/36).

By 1931 the original bus routes had been joined by a service from Oswestry to Babbinswood (in competition with Hampson) and a seasonal express run to Blackpool. The next major change to the stage-carriage side of the business came in 1947 when Lloyd reached an agreement with Crosville to reorganise services between Oswestry and Chirk. Lloyd received a much greater share of market-day (Wednesday/Saturday) workings while Crosville acquired Lloyd's timings on other days of the week. The founder's two sons, William and George, had joined the business by this point and in November 1947 a limited company, JW Lloyd & Sons Ltd, was formed to reflect this fact.

Another Oswestry town service was started in October 1950 and was usually operated by the older Bedfords, while the longer routes to Babbinswood and Chirk were maintained by a 35-seat Maudslay Marathon bus, delivered when new in 1948. The Chirk service proved difficult as it had been revised to operate on only two days a week and yet produced large traffic volumes on those two days. The company's solution was to acquire a very old and cheap double-decker, an ex-London Transport 'STL class' AEC Regent, which arrived in 1953. A second 'STL' was acquired in 1955 and was followed by a wartime Daimler CWA6 utility bus which had been new to Midland Red. The latter machine proved unacceptable to the company's staff and was quickly resold to Bryn Melyn of Llangollen.

In 1958 the first 'STL' was retired after the arrival of a post-war Leyland PD1/Burlingham double-decker from Ribble. The other 'STL' gave way to an ex-Bristol PD1 in 1960 and this latter vehicle would prove to be the last of Lloyd's five double-deckers. In the spring of 1961 the beginning of the end was heralded by the sale of the Babbinswood route, the Blackpool express service, and two Bedford SB coaches to Hampson of Oswestry (qv). The remainder of the business was sold to Crosville in July 1961.

## M & G Motors of Wem

In 1926 Mr Percy Moss began to operate a network of rural market-day services from the small town of Wem. On Tuesday his vehicles ran from Wem to Ellesmere, on Wednesday to Oswestry, and on Friday to Whitchurch. On Thursday two local services connected nearby villages to Wem, while at weekends Mr Moss concentrated on private-hire

and excursion work. Vehicles in use during the 1930s included a Bedford WLB bus, a Crossley acquired from United Automobile Services, and an AEC Regal coach with Harrington bodywork which came from London Transport in 1938 and lasted until 1946. Like many other operators in northern Shropshire the Moss business benefited greatly from the establishment of a large RAF presence in the area during the late 1930s, and in 1943 two OWB utility buses were delivered in recognition of the company's contribution to the local war effort. One of these vehicles maintained a link between Wem railway station and RAF Shawbury while the other operated from RAF Sleap (near Wem) to Shrewsbury.

Early post-war deliveries included two OB/Duple Vista coaches and a nearly-new Guy Arab III coach with Santus bodywork, and these replaced the last of the 1930s machines. In August 1949 Mr Moss combined his operation with that of Mr J Grocott (also of Wem), who contributed a single 1938 vintage Bedford WTB coach to the new limited company, known as M & G Motors (Wem) Ltd. Subsequent deliveries were predominantly of second-hand Bedfords although there were some interesting exceptions such as another Santus-bodied Arab III and a Dutfield-bodied Tilling-Stevens (both acquired from Excelsior of Wrockwardine Wood in 1953, the Tilling-Stevens a former Commercial Motor Show exhibit), a Foden PVSC6 with fully-fronted Metalcraft bodywork purchased third-hand in 1957 and a Plaxton bodied Dennis Falcon L6 which arrived in 1959.

The market-day services were gradually cut back during the 1960s, and by 1971 only the Oswestry and Whitchurch routes remained in operation and most of the six coaches then owned were dedicated to schools contracts and private-hire work. In January 1974 the remaining vehicles and services were sold to Fisher of Bronington and M & G ceased to trade.

## Parish of Morda

The village of Morda (to the south of Oswestry on the main road to Welshpool) has few claims to fame, but for almost six decades its name was familiar to bus enthusiasts as the headquarters of a much-loved independent operator. In 1925 Albert Parish began a market-day service from Llanyblodwel in Denbighshire to Oswestry via

Jones of Market Drayton's first new service bus since 1950 was petrol-powered Bedford SB3/Duple Midland SNT 602 which arrived in February 1959. Five years later it was sold to Banstead Coaches in Surrey. (B Mel Gough Collection)

A Bedford/Duple combination from a later generation, Jones' 1972 YRQ/Viceroy Express XUJ 489K, displays the operator's later blue and white livery which replaced the traditional two-tone blue seen on SNT 602. A rare survivor of its type, the photograph shows it at Kidderminster in October 1994 after purchase for preservation. (Chris Elmes)

Lloyd of Oswestry was famous for its aging (ex-London Transport STL class) AEC Regents. The second of the two examples to see service in the town, BXD 482, arrived in 1955 and was replaced by a comparatively youthful Leyland PD1 acquired from Bristol in 1960. (VC Jones via Peter Harden)

This rather anonymous Bedford SBG/Duple Super Vega, NUJ 313, had been new to Whittle of Highley in 1956 but arrived with M & G of Wem from Jackson of Blackpool in January 1961. It was a regular on M & G's market-day services for more than a decade. (Author's Collection)

Morda using a Ford Model T lorry modified to carry 14 passengers. In 1929 the Ford was replaced by a 20-seat Dennis, and in 1932 this vehicle gave way to a 20-seat Bedford WLB bus. A second market-day service, from Llanfechain to Oswestry, was acquired from H Evans of Llansantffraid in March 1935 along with a Dodge KB coach equipped with 20-seat bodywork by Thurgood. Further coaches soon followed, including a second-hand 20-seat Commer and a brand-new 25-seat Bedford WTB which replaced the earlier Bedford in 1937.

The Dodge was sold in January 1940 and the Commer came to the end of its natural life at the end of 1942, resulting in a need for additional vehicles to cover wartime commitments. In 1941 second-hand examples of the Dodge RBF and Bedford WTB arrived, followed by a Leyland Cub acquired from Arthur of Oswestry in 1942 and then by two Bedford OWB utility buses. Post-war deliveries began in April 1947 with the purchase of a new Bedford OB/Duple Vista coach. A more unusual vehicle arrived in June of 1948 in the shape of a pre-war AEC Regal chassis (new to London Transport) which had received a 31-seat coach body from an unknown source and had been re-registered in Shropshire. In this form it survived for another three years. In 1949 another factory fresh OB/Vista was delivered along with an equally new 33-seat Crossley/Burlingham coach.

From 1950 onwards second-hand vehicles would be the rule, with deliveries in 1952/53 including three more OBs (two coaches and a bus which replaced the surviving OWB) and two Commer Commandos purchased from Creams of Llandudno. Further acquisitions over the next 15 years would include several more OBs (two of them with fully-fronted coach bodywork by Plaxton), Crossley and AEC Regal III coaches, a succession of Bedford SB coaches (plus a solitary Mulliner-bodied bus version), a trio of Commer Avengers and a Thames Trader.

For its first forty years the business had changed very little and had remained a modest enterprise with market-day only stage-carriage services, some schools contracts and private-hire work, and (at the end of 1963) a fleet of six second-hand vehicles. In 1964 this long-established status quo began to change. Albert Parish retired and passed the operation (previously a partnership of the founder and his wife) to his sons, Ivor Tudor Parish and Samuel Henry Roger Parish. The new owners

were the successful applicants for a weekday rail-replacement service from Llanfyllin to Oswestry via Llanfechain and the two market-day routes were absorbed into this new licence. A further development took place at the end of the year when the Parish brothers acquired the business of France of Llanymynech along with a market-day service to Oswestry and yet another Bedford OB. Two years later Parish bought the goodwill of four more market-day services (linking the Crickheath area and Sweeney Mountain to Oswestry) from the Gittins brothers (qv) although on this occasion no vehicles were involved. By 1971 the Parish fleet had almost doubled in size to 11 vehicles, including two AEC Reliances with Plaxton dual-purpose bodywork acquired from Lancashire United Transport to operate the weekday service from Llanfyllin. The partnership also purchased several minibuses to handle small scale private-hire work.

Another notable arrival in 1971 was a Bedford YRQ with Plaxton coach bodywork, the first new vehicle since 1949. The YRQ became the standard vehicle choice for the remainder of the decade apart from minibus deliveries and a pair of second-hand Leyland Leopards from Wallace Arnold. Most of the YRQs were similarly second-hand and included a Willowbrook-bodied bus acquired from Brown of Donnington Wood in 1978 to replace the ex-LUT Reliances on the main stage service.

The end came in early 1982 when the Parish brothers agreed to sell the bulk of the business (all except the minibuses) to Owen's Coaches of Oswestry. The proprietor of this enterprise, Mr Fred Owen, had previously operated from bases in Llangollen, Corwen and Froncysyllte (all in Wales) before moving his business across the border to Oswestry in December 1981. Parish's fleet of well-kept YRQs was soon sold, replaced by a more 'down at heel' mixture of multi-owned vehicles of AEC, Bedford, Ford, Leyland, Seddon and Volvo manufacture. It was a short-lived period of ownership. In September 1983 Mr Owen decided to sell the stage-carriage routes through Morda to Michael Jones of Llansilin in Denbighshire. Mr Jones had entered the local bus industry in 1977 by purchasing services from the Llansilin area to Oswestry from Fred Owen (who had acquired them four years earlier from the Hughes brothers), so the two men were already well acquainted.

In the days before its growth spurt in the mid-1960s, Parish of Morda was a typical Bedford OB operator with market-day only bus routes. OB/Duple Vista LTD 45, a 1949 machine, arrived at Morda in August 1960 from Cowburn of Westhoughton. It lasted until April 1964. (Malcolm Yeomans Collection)

The fully-fronted Plaxton version of the OB was considerably rarer than the 'standard' Duple Vista. An unidentified Shropshire-based Bedford dealership registered ten of them in a block in 1947 and two of the batch later found their way into the fleet of Parish of Morda. This one is DNT 672, operated by them from 1960 to 1962. (Roy Marshall via the Omnibus Society)

Plaxton-bodied Commer Avenger I coach CCB 605 had served operators in Lancashire and Cheshire before continuing its migration southwards to Morda in May 1961. Built in 1950 it gave three years of service to Parish before returning to its native Lancashire with Dex of Rochdale. (Author's Collection)

This 1951 vintage Bedford SB/Mulliner bus, HAW 845, came to Parish from Phillips of Rhostyllen in May 1963. By then petrol-engined buses were an expensive proposition and in November 1965 Parish resold it to a contractor in Birmingham for use as a site office. (Roy Marshall via the Omnibus Society)

The proceeds from the sale of the former Parish services were used to finance a new stage-carriage development. In November 1983 Owen's Coaches began to compete with Robert Lunt's 'Hampson 82' business on the Oswestry-Ellesmere route and on the 'Town' services in Oswestry itself. It was another relatively brief venture. In 1986 these new services were also sold to Michael Jones, and when he ceased trading in 1993 his stage-carriage network passed to another Welsh operator, Tanat Valley. The Owen business survives as a major coach operator in the Oswestry area, but for those of a certain age it is the vehicles of Tanat Valley which serve as a reminder of the pioneering Albert Parish.

## Salopia of Whitchurch

By 1930 there were three stage-carriage operators in the small village of Bronington, Flintshire, just across the border from the Shropshire market town of Whitchurch. The oldest of these businesses was the Chesworth family's Pioneer Motor Service which had developed a sizeable route network from Whitchurch since commencing operations in 1908. William Fisher & Son had been similarly active in the stage-carriage trade since 1920, while Huntbach of Bronington was a relative newcomer having started its market-day only services in 1929.

Whitchurch also had a native contender. In 1916 Mr JR Richards, a local ironmonger, had purchased a 12-seat Wolseley and a 32-seat Selden to operate a contract service from Whitchurch railway station to the major army camp at Prees Heath to the south. This operation came to an end in 1919 and the vehicles were sold, but seven years later the Richards family returned to the bus and coach industry with the acquisition of a 14-seat Commer bus (fleet number 1) and a 20-seat Thornycroft coach (number 2). The new business traded as JR Richards & Sons and was the brain-child of HWB (Harry) Richards, assisted by his brothers Frank and Len. The Commer was mainly used on a Wednesday, Friday and Saturday service which connected Whitchurch with the villages of Tilstock and Whixall, while the Thornycroft found employment on excursions and private-hire work.

Business was buoyant, despite the activities of the Bronington operators, and five more Thornycroft coaches joined the fleet between 1928 and 1934. This rapid expansion was fuelled by Harry Richards' decision to offer extended holiday tours which offered transportation and accommodation at an 'all in' price, a concept which would remain at the heart of the company's operations until the very end. Despite the success of these long-distance offerings the partners were still interested in local stage-carriage work and in October 1934 seized the opportunity to buy the Chesworths' Pioneer Motor Service. Four Chesworth vehicles (two Guys, a Thornycroft, and a Vulcan) were included in the asking price along with routes which passed through several dozen villages and outward to Ellesmere, Market Drayton, Nantwich (in Cheshire), Shrewsbury and Wem. In 1936 the Richards brothers acquired Huntbach of Bronington, along with two vehicles and several market-day licences, leaving Fisher as their only major competitor in the Whitchurch area. The Thornycroft intake in 1936 included three 32-seat buses, two acquired from Sheffield and the other from London Transport, and these vehicles became the mainstays of the vastly enlarged stage-carriage operations.

The trading-name of 'Salopia Saloon Coaches' had been in use for the extended tours since the early 1930s, and in March 1938 this title was formalised when the Richards' partnership became a limited company. In the same year Salopia switched its allegiance from Thornycroft to Dennis, receiving three Lancet 2s of which two were coaches and one a 32-seat bus. Before any more Dennises could be delivered the British government declared war on Germany.

Salopia's extended tour and excursion programmes were suspended for the duration, but the brothers received ample compensation in the form of military contract services from Whitchurch to Prees Heath (reviving their father's original operation) and to the new RAF aerodromes at Tilstock, Ternhill and Shawbury. The company was also active in works services to the Central Ordnance Depot at Donnington and to industrial sites in the other villages to the east of Wellington. A flood of additional vehicles entered the fleet as a result including six new Bedford OWBs and five second-hand Leyland Lions.

The return of peace-time conditions in 1946 brought a rapid revival of the extended tours programme and the scarcity of new vehicles led Salopia to order a variety of types including Bedford OBs, Crossleys, Dennis Lancet J3s and Fodens. In March 1949 the prototype 40-seat Sentinel-Beadle bus was taken into stock and

Barker Street, Shrewsbury, in the early post-war era, and Salopia's 1936 Leyland Cheetah UJ 7432 prepares for its return journey to Whitchurch. The 37-seat coach body (four more seats than was standard) had been created by Santus of Wigan. Note the choice specimens in the background! The Cheetah was sold to a contractor in Chester in September 1951. (Omnibus Society via Tim Butler)

Salopia decided that it liked Fodens. The very first was a PVSC5 with Saunders bus bodywork, DUX 789, which arrived in October 1947. Seen here in Whitchurch bus station in company with other Salopia vehicles, it was withdrawn from service 12 years after delivery and sold to a showman. (Peter Harden Collection)

On the title page we featured one of Salopia's front-engined Foden observation coaches. Here is one of their rear-engined PVRF6 versions, JAW 334 (fleet number 91), a 39-seater delivered in June 1952. Withdrawn after six years with Salopia it was sold (with identical sister vehicle HUJ 996) to Cooper of Gilesgate Moor in County Durham. What a shame that none of these magnificent Whitson-bodied observation coaches survived in preservation. (Ted Jones)

In 1948 Salopia experimented with Crossley chassis, purchasing a 33-seat coach and a 35-seat bus, both with Burlingham bodywork. This is the bus, EUJ 637, and behind it is 1947's Dennis Lancet J3 DUX 785 with identical bodywork. Both vehicles were withdrawn in February 1961. (Author's Collection)

This is the very first diesel-powered Sentinel bus, EUJ 792. Completed in 1948, it entered service with Salopia in March 1949 and after a few teething problems went on to give good service until September 1961. Seen here in Shrewsbury during its heyday, it later became a mobile shop in the same area. (B Mel Gough Collection)

A rare shot of Sentinel STC4/40 demonstrator GUJ 608 in service with Salopia, presumably to provide maintenance cover for the operator's own Sentinel-Beadle. The destination blind reads "on hire to Salopia Saloon Coaches". The vehicle to its left, TRF 993, belonged to Cheshire operator Roberts of Crewe and despite the "Private" blind was employed on Roberts' market day only service to Whitchurch. GUJ 608 is now preserved at the Aston Manor transport museum in Birmingham, repainted into the medium blue and cream colour scheme shown in this photograph. (SNJ White via Peter Harden)

In May 1955 Salopia took delivery of two Commer Avenger III coaches with 41-seat bodywork by Whitson, their last from that manufacturer before standardising on Duple products. MAW 626 (fleet number 102), the first of the pair, went to Belmont of Woodchurch in May 1961. (Author's Collection)

After buying the Sentinel-Beadle integral, Salopia decided to try a Commer-Beadle. MVJ 934, a 42-seat bus, had been new to Yeomans of Canon Pyon in 1955. Salopia bought it in July 1959 and used it until January 1962 when it was sold to Tait of Morpeth. (C Carter via Peter Harden)

The vast majority of Salopia's new coaches from 1954 to 1962 were petrol-powered Bedford SBs with successive variants of Duple Super Vega bodywork. This is the final version of the Super Vega, shown on YAW 171 (fleet number 171), an SB3 41-seater delivered in April 1962 and bound for Brighton. It lasted for three years before being sold with several of its contemporaries to Thomson of Trentham in Staffordshire. (Author's Collection)

In 1963 Salopia switched to the new Duple Bella Vega body, seen here on 1964's AAW 203B showing Folkestone as its destination. Needless to say this was not a stage-carriage service, but Salopia's petrol-powered coaches (including this SB3) were often used on their local network in Shropshire. (Author's Collection)

By 1966 new petrol-engined coaches were virtually extinct, but Salopia kept the faith regardless of the much higher fuel costs. This is FNT 228D, an exceedingly rare Bedford VAM3 with a 45-seat Duple Bella Venture body. This style of bodywork was only produced in 1966, being succeeded by the notoriously fragile Viceroy design in the following year. (Author's Collection)

All subsequent service buses were of Bedford manufacture including six SBs, two J4s and two VAMs. In October 1970 this Willowbrook bodied YRQ, TUJ 921J, arrived. (RF Mack via Chris Elmes)

served on the company's stage-carriage network for more than a decade. A trio of Commer Avenger coaches was tried in 1950, but the major event of that year was the delivery of two Foden PVFE6s with Whitson observation coach bodywork. One of these vehicles, GAW 86, was shipped across the Atlantic to serve as an example of British engineering at the 1950 New York Show.

In 1951 the first of many Bedford SB coaches with Duple Vega bodywork was delivered, a landmark somewhat overshadowed by the purchase of three more Foden/Whitson observation coaches in 1952. These latter vehicles were of the rear-engined PVRF6 variety and one of them, HUJ 996, took part in the 1952 coach rally at Nice in southern France. Despite the indisputable glamour of the observation coaches they were heavy and expensive to operate, and from 1953 until 1965 the vast majority of all new deliveries would be of Duple-bodied (and petrol-engined) Bedford SBs. The exceptions included a handful of smaller Bedfords (some of them with bus bodywork), four more Commer Avengers and a 42-seat Beadle-Commer bus acquired from Yeomans of Herefordshire in 1959. All subsequent bus deliveries would be of diesel-engined Bedfords bodied by Willowbrook and Duple Midland.

From 1966 onwards the Salopia coaching fleet switched from the 41-seat Bedford SB3 to the new 45-seat (and front entrance) VAM3 which also had a petrol engine - by then a rarity. Buses, in contrast, continued to be diesel powered as the poorly patronised rural stage-carriage services needed more economical equipment. The Salopia tradition of using quieter and smoother (but thirstier) petrol engines in its coaches finally came to an end at the beginning of the 1970s as fuel prices increased to unsustainable levels. This change in policy was also motivated by a change in ownership. In 1971 the Richards brothers decided to merge their company with the Gold Case Travel group of Middlesbrough, another leading operator of extended tours. The 'Salopia Gold Case' fleetname was soon adopted for all of the new combination's West Midlands area operations.

In 1977 the Gold Case group was itself taken over by Ellerman Travel, an offshoot of the famous shipping line, and the Shropshire division became Ellerman Salopia. This was to prove even more short-lived, as in August 1979 the coaching interests of Ellerman were sold to the Shearings Ribblesdale group of Altrincham, Greater Manchester. Further amalgamations would see the name change from Shearings-Salopia to Smiths-Shearings in 1985 and then to simply 'Shearings' in 1989. In the same year Shearings acquired Archway Motors (qv), and the richer pickings available in the Telford area led to the decision to close the Whitchurch base and concentrate activities at Shifnal. In February 1992 the entire group's stage-carriage interests were spun off into a separate company, Timeline Travel Ltd, and sold to a management/employee consortium. Six years later, in 1998, any remaining links to Salopia were severed when Timeline Travel's Shropshire division was sold to Midland Red North, itself a subsidiary of the Arriva group.

# Vagg of Knockin Heath

Knockin Heath is a tiny hamlet just off the main road between Oswestry and Shrewsbury and roughly half-way between them. In March 1928 a local resident, Mr Stephen Charles Vagg, took advantage of this central location by purchasing a 14-seat Chevrolet from Brown of Donnington Wood and inaugurating a stage-carriage service which connected the two towns. Despite the not entirely kindly attentions of Midland Red and Oswestry-based JP Arthur (which already ran their own Oswestry-Shrewsbury services) the Vagg initiative proved popular, as it offered lower fares and more convenient timings than the Midland Red offering and a more direct route than the Arthur service. Stephen Vagg's younger brother, John, soon joined the business (he became a full partner in 1934) and by the end of 1930 the fleet included a brand-new 20-seat Chevrolet (which had replaced the original vehicle), a 20-seater Dennis and two small Reo buses. Additional weekday services had also been started which connected Oswestry with Melverley and Shrewsbury with both Kinnerley and Llanymynech, as well as several less frequent routes into Oswestry for market-day traffic.

In 1932 a new 26-seat Commer Corinthian joined the fleet along with another (second-hand) Reo, and by 1934 business was buoyant enough to consider the acquisition of another operator. HC Jones of Oswestry (purchased in January of that year) brought a market-day service from Oswestry to Maesbury Marsh along with a 14-seat

Chevrolet bus. In October 1935 a more substantial service, a weekday operation from Baschurch to Shrewsbury via Stanwardine, was acquired from SC Wells & Son of Baschurch. Vagg's first Bedford, a second-hand WLB, arrived in 1934 and the type's successors (ranging from WTBs and wartime OWBs to post-war OBs and SBs) would dominate the fleet for the next four decades.

Vagg received a total of five new OWBs during the war, a generous allocation by the standards of the time and accounted for by the presence of a large army camp at Nesscliffe, a mile to the south of Knockin Heath. This facility was also served by Arthur of Oswestry which had developed a daily service from its home town to Shrewsbury running slightly to the east of Vagg's route. In August 1947 the Vagg brothers acquired the Arthur business which was slightly larger than their own. The purchase included routes in the Baschurch and Ruyton XI Towns area, a major daily service running northwards from Oswestry to Glynceiriog and Llanarmon (operated jointly with Denbighshire operator LG Phillips), and 12 vehicles – all but four of them Bedfords.

By the end of 1950 the Vagg fleet had grown to include 35 vehicles; 13 Bedfords, 6 Crossleys, 4 Leylands, 3 Commers, 2 Daimlers, 2 Guys, 2 Maudslays and single examples of Albion, Dennis and Thornycroft manufacture. Two of the Leylands were brand-new PD2 double-deckers, acquired for the main Oswestry to Shrewsbury route, while the Thornycroft was a rare post-war double-decker chassis which had been fitted with a single-deck coach body made by Churchill of Norwich. Vagg's first Bedford SB, also fitted with Churchill coach bodywork, arrived from a dealer in July 1951 and would be followed by many more including buses bodied by Duple Midland.

In 1959 the army camp at Nesscliffe closed and the Vagg brothers reversed their previous policy of buying mainly new vehicles. A job-lot of eight OB/Duple Vista coaches and two pre-war Leyland Tiger buses was acquired from Crosville in 1960, and these were followed by six Bristol SC4LK buses from Eastern National in 1964 and no fewer than ten 'normal control' Dennis Falcon buses from Aldershot & District in 1965-67. In November 1967 the aging PD2s were replaced by a pair of slightly younger Weymann bodied AEC Regent IIIs from the City of Oxford fleet, while the 'star' arrival in 1970 was the unique Yeates-

bodied Tiger Cub built for The Delaine of Bourne in 1958.

The early 1970s brought a flotilla of AEC Reliance coaches from Birch Bros and Yelloway, and these were followed by several Bedford VAM and Ford R192 service buses which replaced the Regent III double-deckers. In 1971 Midland Red finally withdrew its (nominally) competing service from Shrewsbury to Oswestry, handing a triumph to the Vagg brothers after 43 years of rivalry on the route. Three years later Stephen and John decided to retire and sold their business to the TE Jones Group, a plant-hire firm based just down the road in Nesscliffe where they occupied a part of the former army camp.

The new owners were intent on developing the coaching side of the Vagg business and most subsequent acquisitions were of Bedford, Ford and Volvo chassis with coach bodywork by Duple and Plaxton. The stage-carriage services were at first modified (with some routes joined into longer and more circuitous 'sweeper' operations) and then drastically reduced except for the main road service between Oswestry and Shrewsbury. An apparent exception to this policy came in 1980 when the business of Hampson of Oswestry was acquired and maintained as a separate subsidiary, but the main attraction could well have been Hampson's express services and other coaching commitments rather than its stage-carriage routes around the Oswestry area and to Ellesmere.

By the beginning of 1982 the Vagg fleet (based at Nesscliffe following the closure of the Knockin Heath premises) included 24 coaches but only one bus, an SB8/Duple Midland vehicle which was already past its optimum sell-by date. In April the Hampson subsidiary lost its separate identity, although few (if any) of its vehicles were repainted into Vagg livery as cash was becoming hard to find. In September the parent TE Jones group went into liquidation and all operations by Vagg came to an end. At the time of its bankruptcy the group had been negotiating to sell off the former Hampson operations and these survived in the ownership of Robert C Lunt. The main road route from Oswestry to Shrewsbury was taken over by Crosville and Midland Red, and several of the routes to outlying villages were also taken up by other operators. It was a shocking and abrupt end for one of Shropshire's finest independent bus operators.

Myers & Bowman, a small bodybuilder based at Distington in Cumberland, specialised in Commer chassis. In September 1948 they delivered this 31-seat Commer Q4 bus to Vagg of Knockin Heath. It was withdrawn in May 1960 and scrapped. (B Mel Gough Collection)

Post-war demand for Bedford OB chassis was so great that some operators acquired 'O series' goods vehicles and had them bodied as PSVs. This 1946 OY lorry, EP 9126, received a 29-seat Mulliner coach body and entered service with Vagg in August 1949. Nine years later it was sold for conversion into a mobile shop. (B Mel Gough Collection)

In 1950 Vagg took delivery of two all-Leyland PD2s, believed to be the only new double-deckers ever operated by a Shropshire independent. This is GNT 220, parked at Knockin Heath alongside ex-Crosville TS7 Tiger/ECW bus BFM 144. (Author's Collection)

Vagg had many rare and unusual vehicles, but this was the rarest of them all. Thornycroft DGN R6 EUJ 787 was built in 1947 as a double-deck chassis. After no orders for this variant were forthcoming it received a Churchill coach body and arrived at Knockin Heath in March 1949. Despite its rarity it enjoyed a full life and was withdrawn in September 1961. Three years later it was scrapped. (B Mel Gough Collection)

Not all of Vagg's purchases were as thrilling as the Thornycroft. This is Bedford SBO/Duple Midland bus MAW 742, bought new in May 1955. It gave a very creditable 16 years of service. (Author's Collection)

Three years later the 'Mini-Me' version of the SBO arrived at Knockin Heath in the shape of this 30-seat Bedford C4Z1/Duple Midland bus, PUX 273. Proving just as durable as its larger cousin, it lasted into the 1970s. (B Mel Gough Collection)

In April 1964 Vagg bought a job-lot of six 35-seat Bristol SC4LK/ECW buses from Eastern National. 601 JPU sits unattended at Knockin Heath with its engine running. A 1957 vehicle, it proved sturdier than the noise and vibration suggested and made it into the 1970s before shaking itself to death. (Author's Collection)

The company's next large batch of second-hand vehicles was even more unusual, consisting of no fewer than ten 'normal control' Dennis Falcon P5/Strachan 30-seat buses acquired from Aldershot & District in 1966/67. The vehicles had been built in 1954 and Vagg withdrew the last of them in January 1970. This one, LOU 69, had gone by February 1969. (Author's Collection)

This 1951 vintage Bedford SB with Duple's original 33-seat Vega bodywork, GVA 462, came to Vagg from Jones of Market Drayton (its third owner) in 1957. It lasted well into the 1970s with its fourth operator and was among the last of its type in regular revenue-earning service on the British mainland. (Author's Collection)

The unique Yeates-bodied Tiger Cub on the right has already been featured on the front cover. Alongside it is 2923 DK, a 1963 AEC Reliance with 36-foot (but only 45-seat) Harrington Cavalier bodywork. As might be suspected from the roof-box destination display and the Rochdale registration the vehicle was new to Yelloway and came to Vagg in May 1971, retaining its luxurious Chapman reclining seats. Both vehicles appear to be on a Llandudno run. (Author's Collection)

# Part Two
# SHREWSBURY AND THE SOUTH

**W**hile the north of Shropshire might be described as 'airfield-flat' the southern half was dominated by a range of substantial hills, most prominent among them Wenlock Edge, Clee Hill and Long Mynd, all of which were visible from the surrounding shires. The valley of the mighty River Severn served as an approximate divider between the two disparate halves of the county, running eastwards from the Welsh border and passing the fortified towns of Shrewsbury and Bridgnorth before turning resolutely southwards to meet its ultimate destination in the Bristol Channel. While airfields were largely unknown (there was a minor base at Condover to the south of Shrewsbury), the rise of Adolf Hitler in the 1930s brought other military installations to southern Shropshire including a massive Royal Navy munitions depot close to the village of Ditton Priors, some considerable distance from the sea but thereby protected from the attentions of the Luftwaffe.

After the Second World War southern Shropshire's economy continued to be driven by agriculture, with sheep-farming prevalent on the hillsides and dairy-farming at lower altitudes. The abundant supply of milk persuaded the English subsidiary of Müller and Company to establish a major dairy products factory in Cleobury Mortimer (the company would later move its British HQ to Market Drayton), while other agriculturally related factories were to be found in Craven Arms (home to the poultry processing plant of JP Wood, later known by the brand-name 'Chuckie Chicken') and in the village of Alscott near Bridgnorth where locally grown sugar beets were processed.

The ancient town of Bridgnorth itself was famous for its attractive mediaeval gates, its ruined castle (including a leaning tower, as close as England came to the more iconic campanile in Pisa) and the cliff railway which made the steep gradient between adjoining points of the town centre less of a challenge. British Railways' decision to abandon their link from Bridgnorth to Kidderminster in the early 1960s brought another opportunity to the area, with the route later reopening under the auspices of the volunteer-run Severn Valley Railway and offering regular steam-train services to an enchanted public.

The original age of steam had also been kind to Shropshire. In 1915 the Sentinel company, then based in Glasgow, had established a second plant in Shrewsbury to help meet the demand for its steam-powered railway engines and road vehicles. The factory soon became the county's largest industrial employer, but the economic depression of the 1930s (along with legislation which favoured the internal combustion engine for road transport) led to the original company's bankruptcy in June 1935. From the ashes there arose the Sentinel Waggon Works (1936) Ltd, with its corporate headquarters in Shrewsbury. The new company continued to produce steam-powered road and agricultural vehicles, but by then it was obvious to one and all that the age of such technology was almost over. In post-war years Sentinel introduced a new range of diesel-powered vehicles in a last desperate attempt to revive the marque. Production came to an end in 1955 after a total of around 1,200 diesel lorries and only 135 buses and coaches had been manufactured.

The Shrewsbury factory was sold to Rolls-Royce and became their Sentinel Division, specialising in the production of engine-parts and machine-tools for 'in house' usage. Those with an interest in the Sentinel story are referred to my earlier book on the subject (Venture Super Prestige series No. 9, co-authored with Ribble and Sentinel expert John Howie) for further details. A gratifying number of Sentinel buses and coaches survive in preservation or in long-term storage at locations ranging from Scotland to Devonshire, although none are currently in their home county of Shropshire which seems like a shame given that at least four of the survivors operated for Brown of Donnington Wood for many years. Local museum curators seem to be more interested in Roman remains and the cast iron industry and should be lobbied incessantly until this situation is rectified!

## Austin of Diddlebury

Edwin P Austin lived in the tiny hamlet of Aston Diddlebury and after the Second World War found work as a part-time driver for the local bus operator, Freeman of Munslow. In late 1949 Alfred Freeman decided to reduce his commitment to stage-carriage work and gave his small team of drivers a 'first refusal' opportunity to buy the unwanted part of the business. Austin was immediately interested and in January 1950 acquired the goodwill of two market-day licences (from Roman Bank to Ludlow on Mondays and from Beambridge to Craven Arms on Tuesdays), a weekday works service to the JP Wood chicken processing plant and a Bedford OB bus from his former employer.

In December 1956 Austin received a licence to operate excursions and tours from the Diddlebury area and in 1959 replaced the OB bus with a coach-bodied example to exploit this new freedom more fully. Six years later this machine gave way to Austin's first 'Big Bedford', a 1951 SB with Duple Vega bodywork, and in August 1966 this was joined by a second vehicle, a 1958 version of the same combination.

The stage service to Craven Arms was withdrawn in the late 1960s, but by way of compensation several schools contracts were acquired which provided work for one of the SBs. In 1972 the older of the pair was replaced by a 1965 model with Plaxton bodywork which

became the front-line vehicle for private-hire and excursion work.

By the summer of 1983 Edwin Austin was eager to retire and in September sold the business to the Bownes family of Ludlow. They abandoned the Austin name and traded as Bowline, continuing the existing stage-carriage operation until January 1987. The service was not registered during the deregulation implementation period, as Bowline chose to concentrate on schools and works commitments and coaching activity in future.

# Boulton of Cardington

Arthur Boulton's wife ran the local shop in the small village of Cardington, to the north of Wenlock Edge. In 1919 he increased his family's business activities by acquiring an Austin Landaulette (basically a large motor-car) and offering private-hire services to the local populace. Two lorry-buses (a Ford Model T and a Willys-Overland) followed, and in their passenger form opened market-day routes from the Cardington area to Much Wenlock (on Mondays), Shrewsbury (on Tuesdays and Saturdays) and Church Stretton (on Thursdays).

Austin of Diddlebury bought this 1945 Bedford OB/Duple bus, CUX 591, from Freeman of Munslow in January 1950 and operated it in a maroon and cream livery. After withdrawal in July 1960 it became a mobile shop. (Author's Collection)

Bedford OB/Duple Vista coach EUJ 832 was new to Boulton of Cardington in 1948 and gave almost 20 years of service to the company. In this early 1960s view at Shrewsbury's Barker Street bus station it sits next to one of Mid-Wales Motorways lowbridge Guy Arabs, Burlingham-bodied CBX 535. (Author's Collection)

In 1953 Boulton acquired the business of Central Garage, Church Stretton, and with it this 1948 Crossley/Whitson coach, EUJ 666. Inevitably referred to by some as 'The Beast', it lasted until August 1965 and presumably met a fiery end with an unknown scrap-dealer. (Roy Marshall via Chris Elmes)

Boulton's first two Bedford SB coaches were Duple-bodied examples purchased from Wellington area operators. The second was 1951 SB/Vega HAW 120 which arrived from AT Brown of Trench in January 1959. It gave more than 12 years of service to its new owners. (Chris Elmes Collection)

Boulton's purchase of Freeman of Munslow in 1959 included two Bedford buses, the OWB pictured earlier and this OB/Mulliner 28-seater, DUJ 185, which had been new to Clun Valley (Parker) in 1947. Seen here parked in a quiet corner of Sunnyside farm, it was withdrawn and scrapped at the end of 1963. (Chris Elmes Collection)

By 1929 these services had attracted enough traffic to justify the purchase of the first 'real' bus, a 14-seat Morris. Over the next ten years this machine was replaced in turn by a 14-seat Chevrolet, a 20-seat Bedford WLB and a 32-seat Leyland Tiger, the latter two vehicles acquired second-hand. Also during the 1930s, Mr Boulton became the licensee of the Royal Oak public-house in the village and the bus company's corrugated iron 'garage' (which had previously stood next to the village shop) was reassembled alongside the pub. The outbreak of war in 1939 brought a marked increase in demand as Boulton's vehicles became regular visitors to the RAF base at Condover and the Royal Navy munitions depot at Ditton Priors.

A Bedford OWB utility bus, allocated during wartime, actually arrived in 1946. This was also the year in which the business moved from the Royal Oak to Sunnyside Farm, taking its corrugated iron shed with it to grace a third site. The OWB was followed by a trio of Bedford OB/Duple Vista in the later 1940s, but activities remained at a very modest level. This began to change in 1951 when a weekday rail-replacement service from Craven Arms to Much Wenlock was awarded to the company, by then a partnership of the founder and his son Arthur John Boulton. Two years later the company acquired the private-hire business of Central Garage in Church Stretton along with a 33-seat Crossley/Whitson coach. The first 'Big Bedford', an SBG/Duple coach acquired from Hoggins of Wrockwardine Wood, came in February 1957, and was followed in January 1959 by another SB from AT Brown of Trench.

By the mid-1960s Arthur John Boulton had become the sole proprietor and his son, John Alan Boulton, the General Manager (he would become a full partner in 1976). Fleet acquisitions during the 1960s included a quartet of second-hand Bedford SBs, two of them from Salopia of Whitchurch which also supplied Boulton's first 45-seat Bedford VAM in November 1970. Later Bedfords included YRQs and VAL70s, one of the latter equipped with unusual Van Hool bodywork.

In 1979 a member of the fourth generation of the family, MJ (Mick) Boulton, had become a private-hire operator in his own right, running a small coach fleet from a base at Harlescott near Shrewsbury. After three years as a sole proprietor

he formed a partnership with HD (Des) Bowen and they adopted the trading name of M & D Travel. Shortly afterwards Arthur John Boulton died, Alan John Boulton decided to retire, and Mick Boulton became the proprietor of the Cardington business as well as a partner in M & D.

Under Mick Boulton's direction the Cardington company updated its coach fleet but also remembered its past by purchasing a 32-year old OB/Vista coach for use on 'heritage' services and 'classic' private-hire work. A second 'heritage' vehicle (a 30-year old SBG/Duple Super Vega) was acquired in 1986 and was later replaced by KNT 780, the late-model Royal Tiger/Burlingham Seagull which had been delivered to Gittins of Crickheath in 1954 and subsequently operated by Vagg of Knockin Heath.

From 1986 onwards Boultons was active in the deregulation arena and successfully tendered for several services far outside of its traditional territory. Mick Boulton's 'other' company, M & D Travel, operated similar contracts from 1992 and both operators used Mercedes-Benz/Optare minibuses on most of their tendered journeys. Vehicles owned by the Cardington company used M & D's premises as a base for their activities in the Shrewsbury area, and in March 1996 M & D Travel was absorbed into the main Boulton business which continued to use the Harlescott depot as an out-station.

In 2003 the family enterprise became Boultons of Shropshire Ltd and continues to operate from Sunnyside under the direction of Mick Boulton and his wife Gill. As the oldest bus operator in Shropshire the company can be proud of its long tradition of service, and even prouder of its ability to adapt and survive where so many have failed.

# Clun Valley of Newcastle

The story of independent bus services in the remote and thinly populated Clun Valley is remarkably complex. In 1923 Geoffrey V Watkins (proprietor of the Ludlow Motor Company which had opened a route from Ludlow to Craven Arms in 1918) began to use the trading-name of Clun Valley Motor Services for a new daily service from Craven Arms railway station to the village of Clun itself. At the end of the 1920s a second operator, Alfred E Parker, opened a service from his home village of Newcastle (further up the valley) to Clun. This was timed to connect with

Watkins' schedule to Craven Arms and also operated under the 'Clun Valley' banner. Parker also began to operate market-day only services from Newcastle to Bishops Castle, Knighton, Ludlow and Shrewsbury, and in 1943 acquired a Clun to Knighton market-day route from Mr TR Whitefoot. The Watkins and Parker businesses gradually moved upwards to 20-seat Bedfords as walkers and other tourists discovered their deeply rural services. One of their customers in the late 1940s, Philip Mountford, recalls that Watkins' regular driver (a Mr Peplow) would board the vehicle with a tray of beer glasses for consumption by both passengers and himself during the journey. The alcohol apparently failed to dim the driver's senses as he was still capable of throwing newspapers into gardens along the way with enviable accuracy!

In January 1952 both of the original proprietors sold their respective businesses. The Watkins portion passed to JW Noakes of Clun, and the Parker services to a partnership of Sydney Theophilus Bradley and Derek Lane. Less than two years later, in October 1953, Mr Noakes sold out to Messrs Bradley & Lane and the Clun Valley Motor Services route network, including a new seasonal express service from Craven Arms to Aberystwyth, was finally unified. The combined fleet included a Bedford WTB which came from Noakes (but had been new to Watkins), four other Bedfords with a Parker pedigree, and a Commer Q2 lorry chassis which carried 14-seat bodywork manufactured by Bradley & Lane in their own garage. All subsequent vehicles were Bedfords (second-hand OBs being followed by second-hand SBs), apart from an Austin CXB coach operated between 1955 and 1959 and the Morris minibuses which replaced the home-made Commer.

Change came again in December 1968 when the partners decided to retire and sold the business to Mr WM (Mervyn) Price whose brother, Geoffrey Price, already ran a garage, car dealership and minibus hire company across the Welsh border in Montgomery. Despite the new management Clun Valley continued to be loyal to the Bedford marque with the exception of a Burlingham-bodied Thames Trader coach acquired from a Birmingham operator in January 1970. In July of the same year the Price brothers bought the four-vehicle coaching fleet of Robinson of Bishops Castle, later renaming it as G & M Coaches and

keeping it separate from Clun Valley. A notable development in 1973 was the purchase of Clun Valley's first new vehicle in a quarter of a century, a 45-seat Plaxton-bodied Bedford YRQ coach which was later preserved as a tribute to the company's history.

In 1976 the Prices decided to amalgamate their various businesses into a single unit, based in Montgomery and (from 1980) using the name Trefaldwyn Motors. Under the Trefaldwyn title new services would be developed, including a through operation from Montgomery to Ludlow, but this later expansion would be by a company based in Wales and thus beyond the boundaries of this book.

# Corvedale of Ludlow

For more than three decades the Corvedale Motor Company of Ludlow was one of Shropshire's leading independent bus operators, but the business's origins lay in Herefordshire to the south where proprietor EE Williams had his ancestral roots. In 1930 Williams began stage-carriage services in the Pontrilas area, southwest of Hereford, and rapidly expanded his network by the acquisition of four other local operators. Further progress was halted by a chronic illness which forced Mr Williams to curtail his business activities, and in October 1936 he sold all but two of his Herefordshire licences to WE Morgan's Wye Valley Motors. Wye Valley had grown at breakneck speed during the 1930s and its services at that time included a trunk route from Hereford to Shrewsbury and a 'feeder' route which brought traffic from Bridgnorth to join the main north-south service at Ludlow. The latter operation was entirely within the county of Shropshire.

By late 1938 EE Williams' health had improved somewhat and he was back in the saddle, operating his two remaining routes with a Bedford WTB coach from his home at Wormelow in Herefordshire. A much greater opportunity was about to present itself. Wye Valley had sold its Hereford-Shrewsbury service to Midland Red in January 1935 and this manoeuvre had left the Ludlow-Bridgnorth route isolated from the rest of the Morgan empire. The Wye Valley proprietor approached Williams and proposed a route-swap. Morgan received the two routes in southern Herefordshire from Williams in exchange for the Shropshire service and two vehicles, a 32-

This Bedford WTB/Duple 26-seater, AAW 14, operated for Clun Valley under the ownership of three proprietors. Delivered to Geoffrey Watkins' Ludlow Motor Co (as seen here) in 1937, it passed to Noakes of Craven Arms in January 1952 and then to Bradley & Lane in October 1953. (JF Higham via Philip Mountford)

Seen at Craven Arms, Bedford OB/Duple bus GAW 464 became a regular vehicle on Clun Valley services in April 1963. New to Whittle of Highley in 1950, it passed to Hastelow of Malvern in January 1959 and then (briefly) to Corvedale of Ludlow in May 1962. Clun Valley kept it until November 1964. (Author's Collection)

seat Dennis Lancet and a 26-seat Reo. Williams retained his WTB which moved northwards with its owner and many of his worldly goods. Premises were acquired at the Kingsley Garage in Ludlow, and in March 1939 the Corvedale Motor Company opened for business under Williams' ownership.

Another Bedford, a 26-seat WTL, was acquired on the second-hand market in May 1939 and was followed by two more Reos. The outbreak of war resulted in a greater variety, with aging vehicles of AEC, Albion, Guy, Lancia, Leyland, Morris and Opel manufacture joining the Corvedale fleet along with four new Bedford OWB utility buses. The solitary Guy came with the business of Cadwallader of Corfton, the first of several operators acquired by Corvedale while one of the Leylands (a Tiger which had been new to North Western) came with the purchase of Holt of Orleton in 1942. The latter acquisition took Mr Williams' growing fleet back into Herefordshire on stage-carriage work.

Traffic on the Corvedale services remained buoyant during the war years and the revenues gained were used to fund further take-overs in the early post-war period. These included Nell Gwynne Coaches (Bodenham, Herefordshire) in 1945, AV Green of Ludlow (1946), Sidney Smith of Bitterley (1948) and Francis Jones of Cleobury North (in 1949). Nell Gwynne's stage-carriage services were resold to Midland Red in June 1947, but the other operators' routes were integrated with those of Corvedale and took the company's vehicles into Ditton Priors and Tenbury Wells on a daily basis. Longer distance services were inaugurated during 1949, connecting Ludlow to Much Wenlock (daily), Worcester (on weekdays) and Walsall (on summer Saturdays and Sundays). Much of this new mileage replaced withdrawn passenger railway services.

In the late 1940s EE Williams decided to broaden the scope of his company by beginning to trade in second-hand buses and coaches. To differentiate between his own vehicles and those acquired for resale, fleet numbers began to be used for the 'active' fleet, although it was far from unknown for numberless machines to be hurriedly pressed into service. New vehicles received during the late 1940s included ten bonneted Bedfords (six coaches and four buses) and two Crossleys (a bus and a coach). In late 1950 Mr Williams decided to order two new

underfloor-engined Sentinel STC4 buses for his longer range services. The Sentinels arrived in the Spring of 1951 but their mechanical teething problems resulted in low utilisation and the kind of unexpected expenses which Corvedale could ill afford. Both had gone by early 1954 and the financial difficulties caused by their introduction had forced Mr Williams to sell some of his most prestigious routes to Midland Red in May 1953, including the original service to Bridgnorth and the more recent operations to Much Wenlock, Worcester and Walsall. By this drastic butchery the balance of the business (including a Ludlow town service, weekday routes to Cleobury North and Ditton Priors and a dozen or so market-day runs) managed to survive the crisis. Some recompense for this shrinkage came in 1954 when Corvedale acquired services from Ludlow and Craven Arms to Knighton from the Yeomans family.

Despite this diet of humble pie the fleet was still expanding in size. Bedfords (including the larger SB model) continued to be the mainstay of operations for the rest of the 1950s although there were also significant numbers of AEC Regals including a batch of pre-war examples acquired from Halifax. Maudslay Marathon IIIs were also briefly popular as they used the same running units as post-war Regals. By 1960 Bedford SBs out-numbered Bedford OBs for the first time, although the latter type would remain in the fleet for another decade.

In October 1960 the two routes to Knighton were sold to Griffiths of Leintwardine (trading as Teme Valley), but the revenues thus lost were soon regained by the acquisition of Mr F Yarranton's Tenbury Wells Motor Service in June 1961. This brought a new link between Ludlow and Tenbury Wells and a market-day service from Tenbury Wells to Bromyard which was wholly within Worcestershire. Mr Yarranton had originally been a partner in the Yarranton Brothers business (based at Eardiston) before striking out on his own by acquiring Critchley of Tenbury Wells.

By 1961 the need to replace the remaining bonneted Bedfords with something more modern (and diesel-powered) had been recognised. Mr Williams startled the horses by purchasing four 'GS class' Guy Vixen Specials from London Transport, among the first of these robust 26-seat vehicles to enter service in the independent

Corvedale's 1943 Bedford OWB/Duple utility bus CWV 964 came from Giles of Cricklade (Wiltshire) in August 1950. Its fate remains unknown but it gave at least seven years of service to the Ludlow company. (Peter Harden Collection)

Bedford OB/Mulliner bus GAW 759 had been new to Whittle of Highley in 1950 and was sold to Corvedale (as seen here, sandwiched between two coach bodied OBs) in March 1952. In October 1954 they resold it to Hoggins of Wrockwardine Wood. (SNJ White via Peter Harden)

Not all of Corvedale's second-hand purchases were Bedfords. In 1950 the company acquired four pre-war AEC Regal buses from Halifax. Roe-bodied JX 6579, seen in Ludlow, was the final survivor of the quartet when withdrawn in 1955. It then passed to Airtech of Haddenham as a staff bus. (SNJ White via Peter Harden)

Corvedale occasionally bought some new vehicles such as 29-seat Bedford C5Z1/Duple Super Vista coach TUX 416, delivered in November 1959. In April 1962 the vehicle was sold to Yarranton Bros of Eardiston (Peter Harden Collection)

Corvedale's first Bedford SB bus was delivered new in 1954 and was followed by a variety of second-hand examples. This 1958 SB1/Duple Midland, CSX 229, arrived in Ludlow in September 1962. Its original owner, Scottish Oils, had used it for staff transport. In February 1970 Corvedale sold it to Vagg of Knockin Heath. (Author's Collection)

Another purchase in September 1962 was this much rarer bird, a petrol-powered SB3 with 41-seat bus bodywork by Owen. XYL 219 had also been a staff bus when new in 1959. In March 1964 it passed from Corvedale to Kearsey of Cheltenham. (Peter Harden Collection)

Ex-London Transport GS type MXX 372 was previously illustrated on page 15, still in LT livery. Here it is after repaint into Corvedale's standard colour scheme, apparently awaiting a dentist, as hungry as a hippo, or – more likely – awaiting attention to its Perkins engine. Most second owners of GS type vehicles found these engines to be far more unreliable than the Bedford petrol units fitted to the immortal OB. (Peter Harden Collection)

Bedford OB/Duple Vista coach GCY 153, built in 1949, was acquired by Corvedale in May 1963. It only stayed for two months before resale, but this was long enough for it receive fleet-number 11 and to have its photograph taken. (Author's Collection)

sector. Three further 'GSs' were acquired in 1963 but Corvedale continued to hedge its bets by purchasing more second-hand OBs, along with a variety of small Bedfords of more recent manufacture including C5, J4 and VAS models. The Bedford SB remained the standard 'full size' vehicle until partially superseded by 45-seat VAMs (and a single three-axle VAL) from 1966 onwards.

In 1965 EE Williams decided to retire and sold his company to the Yeomans family of Canon Pyon, Herefordshire. The new owners maintained Corvedale as a separate unit, renaming it as Corvedale Travel in November 1967. Less than two years later, in June 1969, Corvedale was sold again, to the Whittle family of Highley (qv). Whittle had already (in 1964) acquired M & M Coaches of Kidderminster which operated stage-carriage services in the area between Cleobury Mortimer and Tenbury Wells, immediately to the east of the Corvedale network. Both M & M and Corvedale retained their own separate identities until 1981 when they were merged into the main Whittle operation.

## Davies of Acton Burnell

This business was founded in the mid-1920s by Albert Davies and Mr W Preece, initially as a light haulage contractor. The first bus, a 14-seat Chevrolet, arrived in September 1928 and was used to open a regular service from Kenley and Acton Burnell to Shrewsbury. By the end of 1931 Mr Preece had left the partnership which continued to prosper under the sole direction of Albert Davies. The Chevrolet was followed by a pair of Bedfords, a 20-seat WLB bus and a 26-seat WTB coach, and during the 1930s several other small businesses were acquired along with more services from the local villages to Shrewsbury.

Both of the Bedfords had gone by the end of 1943, their duties usurped by a single second-hand AEC Regal 4 allocated to Davies by the government. In 1947 this stop-gap wartime vehicle was sold and replaced by a brand-new Commer Commando with 29-seat coach bodywork by Myers & Bowman, and in the same year a formal company, Albert Davies (Transport) Ltd was registered to continue the business. Two years later a major schools contract was secured and the fleet tripled in size. The new vehicles were another Commando coach (with Harrington

bodywork) and a Crossley with a 33-seat coach body by Plaxton.

A third Commer Commando (a second-hand Harrington-bodied example) arrived in June 1955 and replaced the Myers & Bowman specimen which had developed major structural problems. The two surviving Commandos and the Crossley would soldier on until July 1965 when all PSV operations came to a sudden end. Davies's stage-carriage services were incorporated into those of their near neighbour Boulton of Cardington (qv) and the two Commers were sold to a scrap-dealer who dismantled them on site and burned the remains. His offer for the Crossley was less generous, and as a result of his stinginess this magnificent vehicle survives in preservation. Still in the operator's traditional livery it serves as a lasting reminder of this otherwise forgotten bus company.

## Foxall of Bridgnorth

In the late 1920s there were two separate Foxall family coaching businesses in Bridgnorth, both operating vehicles of Guy manufacture. Mr D Foxall traded from West Castle Street and ceased operations in the early 1930s. Mr R Foxall and his sons Harold and Sidney were based on Friar Street and their business outlasted that of their relative by more than forty years.

Private-hire and excursion work provided the bulk of Foxall & Sons revenue throughout the company's history, although a seasonal express service from Bridgnorth to Blackpool was licensed by the new Traffic Commissioners in 1931 and in March 1932 a weekday operation from Bridgnorth to the village of Ditton Priors was also approved. Bedfords replaced Guys in the second half of the 1930s, and during the Second World War two Bedford OWB utility buses were allocated to Foxalls. These were employed on the route to Ditton Priors (which had become more important due to the presence of a Royal Navy establishment in the area) and on a new service which connected Bridgnorth to Stanmore (site of an RAF camp) and Halfpenny Green aerodrome. The section of this route between Bridgnorth and Stanmore continued after the war, latterly available to the general public.

Post-war purchases were mostly new and almost exclusively of Bedford manufacture, an exception being a Burlingham-bodied Crossley

Albert Davies' Commer Commando/Harrington coach FAW 123 is seen in Shrewsbury on the weekday stage service. The vehicle had been new to Hoggins of Wrockwardine Wood in February 1949 and passed to Davies in June 1955. Ten years later the PSV side of the business ceased to trade and FAW 123 was scrapped on site at Acton Burnell. (Roy Marshall via Chris Elmes)

Foxall of Bridgnorth bought this 1951 Bedford OB/Duple bus when new from a Wolverhampton dealer, hence the registration HUK 328. Seen here in Bridgnorth in Foxall's attractive light blue livery, it lasted until March 1965 and then saw further service with a contractor in Warwick. (Roy Marshall via the Omnibus Society)

delivered in 1949. All were coaches apart from a second-hand Bedford OB bus acquired in August 1951 to replace the wartime OWBs. This vehicle was usually to be found on the Stanmore route while the Ditton Priors service was operated by coach-bodied OBs.

Despite the gradual rundown of the Royal Navy facility close to the village the Ditton Priors operation remained viable until the early 1970s, while the service to Stanmore ended in February 1968. On 17th January 1976 the Foxall business, by then operating eight vehicles (all of them coaches) was acquired by the Whittle family of Highley (qv) and gradually disappeared into the larger company.

## Lewis of Tankerville

In September 1947 Mr TW (Walter) Lewis and Mr W Preece, trading as L & P Coaches, acquired the business of Mr H Wood of Clun. The deal included a 1930 vintage Dennis 14-seater and a contract to provide schools services in the Bishops Castle area. Mr Preece had previous experience in the industry from an earlier involvement with Albert Davies of Acton Burnell (qv). The original Dennis bus was supplemented, and later replaced, by a succession of five small Bedfords (three of them with bus bodywork) and two pre-war Dennis Lancet coaches.

In 1953 Mr Preece sold his share in the partnership to Walter Lewis and the trading name was altered accordingly to Lewis's Coaches. Bedfords remained as the first choice of equipment but some variety was provided by single examples of Austin, Crossley and Dodge manufacture. All vehicles purchased after 1951 were coaches, reflecting the gradual shift from schools contracts to more general private-hire work.

The Lewis business had taken up residence in Tankerville, a short distance from the Montgomeryshire border, and in 1962 the proprietor decided to acquire the stage-carriage services of William H Hailstone of Churchstoke, an English village marooned across the boundary in Wales and thus in the North West Traffic Area. Hailstone's surviving vehicle, a Thurgood-bodied Bedford OB, proved unattractive to the buyer and Lewis replaced it with two relatively new Bedford SB coaches. The services acquired were market-day runs from the Churchstoke area to Shrewsbury (on Tuesdays and Saturdays) and to Welshpool

(on Mondays and Saturdays) and these continued into the 1970s despite a steadily declining level of patronage. In April 1974 the business was acquired by a neighbouring operator, Minsterley of Stiperstones (qv) and Walter Lewis retired.

## Minsterley of Stiperstones

In early 1948 Messrs AJ (Albert) Evans and JE (John) Lewis bought a ten year old 35-seat Tilling-Stevens bus and began to offer private-hire services from the village of Stiperstones, to the west of Long Mynd. Their initial vehicle proved to be short-lived as the Tilling-Stevens suffered mechanical failure within a matter of months and was subsequently scrapped. In the following spring they tried again, this time with a third-hand Bedford OWB utility bus, and strengthened their business plan by acquiring two stage-carriage services from Mr WJT Swain in the neighbouring village of Bog Mines.

William John Thomas Swain had started operations between The Bog and Shrewsbury in the late 1920s and this daily service, along with a market-day run to Bishops Castle and an excursions and tours licence, had provided him with a living for two decades. No vehicles were involved in the sale to Evans & Lewis as Mr Swain's regular workhorse, a pre-war Bedford WTB, was older than the OWB which they already owned.

With the OWB committed to their new stage services the partners needed a second vehicle to develop the excursions, tours, and private-hire side of their business. In February 1951 a late-model OB/Duple Vista coach was acquired, no doubt at an attractive price as most buyers preferred to order the new SB model. An identical second-hand OB arrived in May 1952 and at around that time the trading name of the Minsterley Motor Company came into use, replacing the 'Cosy Coaches' fleet-name used on the 1951 vehicle.

A brand-new 35-seat Burlingham-bodied SB coach was delivered in 1953 and was followed by a second-hand Crossley/Plaxton coach which replaced the OWB on the Shrewsbury service. The Crossley was destined to become the only non-Bedford acquired between 1949 and the early 1980s, and only lasted for two years before resale to Lewis of Tankerville (qv).

In March 1956 John Lewis decided to sell his share in the business and Albert Evans became the sole proprietor. From 1956 until 1971 all

Walter Lewis of Tankerville liked his Bedford SB coaches. The first to arrive was NWR 263, a Yeates Riviera-bodied SBG built in 1954. Lewis acquired it in November 1959 from Whippet of Hilton and withdrew it in August 1962. (Roy Marshall via Chris Elmes)

SBG/Duple Super Vega NUN 167, new in 1956, came to Walter Lewis in January 1962 and is seen in Barker Street, Shrewsbury, alongside a Mid-Wales Motorways' Sentinel. The Bedford stayed at Tankerville until September 1964. (Brian Botley via Chris Elmes)

This was Lewis's Tankerville headquarters. Poking out of the garage is 1959 built SB3/Super Vega MTK 333 which replaced NUN 167 in September 1964 and survived into the 1970s. (Malcolm Knight)

Minsterley Motors acquired this 1950 Bedford OB/Duple Vista coach, FTH 201, from West Wales of Tycroes in March 1959. It was eventually withdrawn in November 1970. (Roy Marshall via Chris Elmes)

The next vehicle to join the Minsterley fleet was a brand-new Bedford SB1/Duple Super Vega coach, UAW 883, which arrived in January 1960. Seen here in Shrewsbury alongside two Vagg buses and a Watneys lorry, it was traded in for another new SB/Duple coach in May 1962. (Roy Marshall via Chris Elmes)

purchases (both new and second-hand) were Bedford SB variants except for a used OB/Vista coach acquired in 1959 and a 45-seat VAM/Duple coach bought new in March 1966. The Friday-only route to Bishops Castle (inherited from Swain) was withdrawn in 1965 due to lack of demand, but the main service to Shrewsbury continued to prosper.

Little changed during the 1970s although the new Bedfords included a 45-seat YRQ/Duple Viceroy Express with 'bus grant doors' for stage-carriage work and a second-hand arrival was an SB5/Duple Midland bus acquired from Shropshire County Council. The company also acquired some additional stage services with the purchase of Lewis of Tankerville (qv) in 1974. A pair of second-hand 53-seat YRT coaches came in 1981, but the following year would produce some changes of far greater significance. In early 1982 the business became a limited company (under the Minsterley name) and acquired the Bishops Castle operations of Valley Motor Services (qv). The purchase included a daily service from Bishops Castle to Shrewsbury, market-day runs to Craven Arms, Ludlow, Newtown and Welshpool, four Ford/Duple coaches and three Ford/Willowbrook buses. Minsterley more than doubled in size as a result and became the largest independent bus operator in south-western Shropshire.

Minsterley continued to grow during the 1980s and by the time of deregulation had 19 vehicles in its fleet. Many of the recent acquisitions were still Bedfords (including a YRT bus with 53-seat Alexander Y-type bodywork which came from Lothian Transport), but the sudden influx of Fords from Valley had broken the monopoly and the coaching roster also included a new DAF and a third-hand Leyland Leopard (which had the coach version of Alexander's Y-type design). All seemed well but deregulation brought inevitable financial problems for a 'deeply rural' business such as the Minsterley Motor Company.

In January 1989 the original limited company went into voluntary liquidation and was replaced by Hillside Coaches Ltd which continued to trade under the Minsterley name. After only six months Hillside also entered administration and the Minsterley name and assets passed to a third company, Oakrim Ltd. Four years later the business's debts were successfully cleared and ownership returned to a partnership of the Evans

family. Finally, in May 2001, the partners created a new limited company, Minsterley Motor Services Ltd, which survives to the present day.

In 2003 the business took delivery of three brand-new Volvo B7RLF/Wright 44-seat buses to operate the local service network. An informative website includes timetables for all of the company's bus services, a development beyond the imagination of its founders back in 1949, and Minsterley (despite its period of financial shakiness in the early 1990s) survives as a shining example of a successful rural bus operator.

# Valley of Bishops Castle

In November 1957 RW (Bob) Carpenter, one of the pioneers of the southern Shropshire bus industry, sold his eponymous enterprise (which also traded as Valley Motors) to the Lewis family. Carpenter had started operations from Churchstoke in Montgomeryshire to Shrewsbury in 1929 using the trading name of 'Hope Valley Services'. By 1933 the business had moved across the border to Bishops Castle and Carpenter had acquired premises at the former railway station in that town, closed to passenger traffic in 1932. His operations at that time included a daily service to Shrewsbury and two local routes on Fridays which was Bishop Castle's market-day. In the pre-war era the company's fleet was predominantly of Chevrolet and Bedford manufacture but there were also several second-hand Tilling-Stevens buses, one of which came from Southdown via Worthen & District. Carpenter's main competitors on the Shrewsbury road were the businesses of James Rose and Samuel Roberts. Rose died in 1938 and in September 1939 his widow sold his company to Carpenter. The deal included the Shrewsbury route, market-day runs to Craven Arms, Ludlow, Montgomery and Newtown, and several vehicles. Two years later Carpenter also acquired the Roberts business which brought a further market-day service to Welshpool. Wartime deliveries to operate this growing network included a second-hand Daimler CP6 (from Central SMT) and several Bedford OWB utility buses.

Post-war purchases were mostly of Bedford origin although a Churchill-bodied Commer Avenger arrived in 1949 to provide an interesting contrast to the hordes of OBs. The business expanded again in 1951 when Carpenter bought a daily Bishops Castle to Craven Arms service from

Bedford OB/Duple bus CUX 804, built in 1946, was in the Valley Motor Services fleet when William Lewis and his family bought the company from Bob Carpenter in November 1957. Its fate remains unrecorded. (JF Higham)

Commer Avenger I/Churchill coach FNT 946 had been new to Bob Carpenter's business in 1949 and it also passed to Valley's new owners. Apparently unimpressed they sold the vehicle to Griffiths (Teme Valley) of Leintwardine in June 1958. (Roy Marshall via Chris Elmes)

In November 1958 this 1952 Leyland Royal Tiger/Plaxton Venturer coach, PTD 489, arrived from Moore of St Anne's. Seen here in Shrewsbury between a Mid-Wales Sentinel and an Austin FX3 taxi, the vehicle stayed with Valley for two years before sale to Foster of Dinnington, near Sheffield. (Chris Elmes Collection)

In May 1965 Valley acquired this 1954 Leyland Tiger Cub with rare Mann Egerton Sandringham bodywork, NWX 442. New to the famous fleet of Samuel Morgan (Blue Line) in the Doncaster area, it arrived in Bishops Castle from intermediate owner Parfitt of Rhymney. It lasted until May 1970 and was then (tragically) scrapped. (RF Mack via Geoff Mills)

An even rarer vehicle came to Bishops Castle in August 1965 when Valley bought Seddon Mark 11/Duple Midland bus FHL 987. Built in 1954 as a one-off for West Riding (in the hope of a major order which never materialised), the vehicle passed to Rowe of Cudworth in 1963 before its migration to Shropshire. It was never very active with Valley and after withdrawal in November 1967 it vanished without trace. (Chris Elmes Collection)

In 1970/72 Valley acquired two new Ford R192/Willowbrook service buses and in 1975 they were joined by KUX 321P, a slightly larger Ford R1114/Willowbrook with 54 seats. In 1982 the Bishops Castle part of the Valley business (including the three Ford buses) passed to Minsterley Motors. (Chris Elmes)

the Yeomans family. This route had been started by the railway company to replace its passenger trains and had then passed to Bishops Castle Motor Services, WA Thomas's Plowden Valley Motors and Yeomans before arriving in Bob Carpenter's impressive domain.

When Carpenter decided to sell out to William E Lewis and family in 1957 his fleet included the Commer Avenger, six Bedford OBs (one of them a bus version) and a 1951 Bedford SB/Duple Vega coach. The new owners replaced the vehicles' almost universal 'RW Carpenter Motor Services' titles with the 'Valley Motors' branding which had also been used (sporadically) by the previous proprietor. One vehicle which escaped this change was the Avenger which was quickly traded in against a Leyland Royal Tiger/Plaxton coach. A less glamorous arrival in 1959 was a five year old Bedford SB/Duple Midland bus from Corvedale of Ludlow (qv).

In March 1961 the Lewis family partnership gave way to a limited company, Valley Motor Services (Bishops Castle) Ltd. Deliveries during the 1960s included three Thames Trader/Duple coaches in 1963 (two new, one second-hand), an Albion Aberdonian/Plaxton coach acquired from a dealer in 1964, and a pair of extremely rare vehicles bought with the stage-carriage services in mind. The first of these (acquired in May 1965) was a Leyland Tiger Cub with Mann Egerton Sandringham bodywork, the other (which arrived in August of the same year) a Seddon Mk 11 with Duple Midland bus bodywork. Less than a dozen Sandringham bodies were built in 1954-56, while the Seddon Mk 11 (built in 1954) was the only one of its type to be sold as a bus in the UK market. The Sandringham gave five years' service as Valley's front-line vehicle, while the Seddon proved less useful and spent a lot of its time in the depot yard before being sold for scrap in late 1967. The Sandringham's eventual replacement in 1970 was a brand-new 45-seat Ford R192/Willowbrook service bus. A similar machine was delivered in 1972 and was followed by a larger 54-seat Ford R1114/Willowbrook in 1975. Fords were also favoured for the coaching fleet in the 1970s and soon replaced the remaining Bedfords.

The purchase of a third service bus in 1975 was prompted by the acquisition of TJ Green's Worthen Motorways (qv) in September 1974. This gave Valley a second daily service into Shrewsbury (from Montgomery in Wales) and also brought five more coaches into the fleet, two Bedfords and three more Fords. The 1970s might well be described as the 'heyday' of the Valley business, but the following decade would witness the company's piecemeal demise.

In October 1980 the original (1961) limited company became a subsidiary of a new corporate entity, Valley Motors (Haulage) Ltd. The Lewis family had continued in their traditional trade after purchasing Bob Carpenter's bus interests and operated several lorries from a site in Shrewsbury, but the change in their company hierarchy proved ominous. In January 1982 Valley sold its Bishops Castle services, including all of those purchased from Bob Carpenter, to the Minsterley Motor Company of Stiperstones (qv). Valley kept its haulage business, the Shrewsbury to Montgomery service acquired from Worthen Motorways and five Ford coaches. With the Ford buses gone (to Minsterley) Valley needed suitable equipment for the Montgomery route and quickly acquired two 53-seat Bedford YRT/Willowbrook buses from United Counties. These vehicles remained in NBC leaf green and white livery, a sign perhaps that the Lewis family was losing interest in its surviving PSV operations. No further vehicles were purchased and in May 1986 the rump of Valley Motor Services was sold to Mr David A Pye of Worthen. The new proprietor was required to relinquish the Valley name (still used by the haulage company) and traded as Worthen Travel.

The vehicles acquired from Valley (the two Bedford buses and five Ford coaches) were rapidly chased out by second-hand coaches of Bedford, DAF and Ford manufacture purchased by Mr Pye. By the end of the 1980s the only bus-seated vehicle in the Worthen Travel fleet was a Bedford OB, acquired from a preservation group in 1987 to operate a 'heritage' service in the Ironbridge area. For an all too brief period it served as a reminder of a bygone era when Bob Carpenter and his fleet of bonneted Bedfords had been a force to be reckoned with in the rural south-west of the county.

# Whittle of Highley

The colliery village of Highley lies to the west of the River Severn, roughly half-way between the two local market towns of Bridgnorth (in Shropshire) and Kidderminster (in Worcestershire).

Whittle of Highley took delivery of two new Daimler CVD6/Willowbrook service buses in 1948 and kept them until 1956. Seen here is ENT 791. After withdrawal by Whittle the dark blue and red Daimlers were exported to an operator in the Canary Islands. (Peter Harden Collection)

Leyland/MCCW HR40 Olympic KOC 241 served briefly as a demonstrator before sale (along with sister vehicle KOC 242) to Whittle in early 1950. The Olympics found few friends at Highley and in November 1953 they were sold to Llynfi of Maesteg. (Chris Warn Collection)

Whittle of Highley had many Royal Tigers, but only one of them was a bus. All-Leyland KAW 677, new in 1954, is seen on the Kidderminster service. Note the change of fleetnames from 'Whittle's' to 'JT Whittle & Son'. In 1960 the vehicle was sold to Eynon of Trimsaran. (Roy Marshall via the Omnibus Society)

From 1960 onwards Whittle's stage-carriage services were operated by brand-new coaches such as Thames Trader/Burlingham Seagull 60 UAW 983, seen here on private-hire duties in London. Delivered in January 1960, it was sold in March 1961 to a Scottish operator. (Chris Elmes Collection)

A regular service between the two towns began in the Worcestershire Motor Transport era, swiftly passing to Midland Red, but this connection made use of the main road to the east of the Severn and was of no use to the villagers of Highley.

In 1930 Mr James T Whittle (who had previously operated a pony and trap for the coalmine with the help of his two young sons, George and Wesley) decided to enter the bus industry and began a weekday service from Highley to Bridgnorth with a 14-seat Ford Model T. The new service was a huge success and the Ford was followed by a Chevrolet, a 20-seat GMC coach, and then a 14-seat Bedford WHB bus. In 1932 Whittle purchased a second route, from Highley to Bewdley and Kidderminster, from F & L Harper of the latter town. A second-hand 32-seat Crossley bus was acquired to operate this service and was followed by a new 20-seat Bedford WLB bus in 1933 and by an equally new 26-seat Leyland Cub coach in April 1935. Later in the same year Whittle made a further commitment to the coaching market by acquiring the remainder of the Harper brothers business, including a seasonal express service from Kidderminster to Llandudno and assorted excursions and tours licences. No vehicles were involved in this transaction, but before the start of the 1936 summer season Whittle acquired two more new coaches, a 26-seat Bedford WTB and a 32-seat Daimler CP6. Six more new coaches would join the fleet before the outbreak of war along with three WTBs with lorry-bus bodywork by Greenhous of Shrewsbury (Whittle still hauled coal as a side-line), among the last examples of this kind of hybrid vehicle for an English operator. The disparity in capital expenditure was also an indication that the main focus of the business had shifted from the stage-carriage routes (marketed as 'Highley Bus Services') to the more profitable coaching market.

During the Second World War the stage services continued and were supplemented by works journeys to military and industrial locations and by 'Forces Leave' express services to various British cities. Four Bedford OWB utility buses were allocated to Whittle along with six second-hand Bedford and Leyland coaches. The Bedford motif continued when the war ended with no fewer than 21 new OB coaches arriving in 1946-49 along with smaller numbers of AEC Regal IIIs, Crossley SD42s, Dennis Lancet J3s and Maudslay Marathons. This

massive investment was justified by an expansion of the excursions and extended tours business and by new seasonal express services from Bridgnorth to Torquay and Weston-super-Mare and from Worcester to Blackpool and Llandudno, all four of these operations running via pick-up points in Highley, Kidderminster and Bewdley.

The bus fleet was rejuvenated in the post-war era by a handful of Bedford OBs and a pair of Daimler CVD6s with 35-seat Willowbrook bodywork. In 1950 most of the new coaches were Daimler CVD6s and Leyland Tigers with fully-fronted Burlingham Sunsaloon bodywork, but the same year witnessed the arrival of the first underfloor-engined vehicles in the shape of two 40-seat Leyland/MCCW Olympic buses which had briefly been used as company demonstrators and thus carried Birmingham registrations. These were resold to a Welsh operator at the end of 1953 but served as the forerunners for a fleet of Leyland Royal Tiger/Burlingham Seagull coaches delivered in 1951-54. There was also a solitary (all-Leyland) Royal Tiger bus, delivered in 1954 along with a 40-seat Bedford SBO/Duple Midland bus. Both of these vehicles could often be found at Weston-super-Mare on summer weekends, acting as rather uncomfortable duplicates to the coaching fleet. The SBO bus was sold in 1956 along with the pair of CVD6 buses, leaving the stage services in the hands of the Royal Tiger bus and two surviving OBs with bus bodywork. By the end of 1960 this trio had also departed and Whittles had become an all-coach fleet. The use of luxurious coaches on local bus services brought few complaints from passengers.

James T Whittle had been the sole proprietor of the business from 1930 until 1954 when he formed a partnership which included his sons, George and Wesley. In 1964 the founder decided to retire and passed ownership to a new partnership, headed by George and including George's wife, Dorothy, and son, Ronald. By that time the Whittles' enterprise was already one of the largest coach operators in the West Midlands, but was destined to become even more important as a result of later acquisitions. In 1965 the Whittle family took control of M & M Coaches of Kidderminster (which operated stage-carriage services in Shropshire from a base at Cleobury Mortimer) and in 1969 the Corvedale Motor Company of Ludlow (qv) was acquired from the Yeomans group. The following decade, when Ronald Whittle took control, saw the acquisitions of Foxall & Sons of Bridgnorth (qv) in 1976 and Morris Coaches (also of Bridgnorth) in 1979. Morris had acquired the former Foxall route from Bridgnorth to Stanmore in March 1968 and had also started a weekday service to Sutton Maddock in 1972.

In 1981 the surviving subsidiaries (Corvedale Travel and M & M) were merged into the main Whittle business. This created a fleet of 54 vehicles and all except for two minibuses were full-size coaches, mainly Bedfords with Duple and Plaxton bodywork. A few were equipped with 'bus grant doors' to make them suitable for use on the stage-carriage network. As a nationally renowned coaching company Whittles had little to fear from the deregulation process and in October 1980 took advantage of the relaxed rules by opening an express service from Kidderminster to London. When local bus services were deregulated in 1986 Whittles retained most of its existing network and gained some new routes through the tendering process. On the debit side the premises in Cleobury (Ex-M & M) and Ludlow (ex-Corvedale) were closed and the company's activities centralised at a new depot in Kidderminster. It was thus no longer a Shropshire independent.

In 2004 the Whittle family, by then in its third 'bus owning' generation, sold the business to the EYMS Group which has maintained it since then as a separate unit under the Whittle Bus & Coach brand-name. The company continues to be a major provider of local bus services in south-eastern Shropshire and northern Worcestershire, although most of its fleet can usually be found in more distant and exotic locations.

## Williamson of Shrewsbury

In 1919 Joseph and Eva Williamson bought a canvas-roofed Ford Model T lorry-bus and started a regular service between Shrewsbury and the village of Pulverbatch in the hills to the south, using the trading-name of Direct Motors. A second 14-seat Model T with a rigid roof followed, and in 1922 was superseded by the first purpose-built bus, a 32-seat Daimler which received the name 'Maid of the Mountains'. A similar vehicle was added to the inventory in 1925 and opened further bus services to the villages of Rodington and Withington, to the east of Shrewsbury, with some journeys continuing to Wellington.

The Daimlers proved to be rather too large for the amount of traffic on offer, and in January 1926 the second machine was replaced by a 14-seat Willys-Overland, itself replaced by a Chevrolet in the following year when Eva Williamson left the partnership to form her own company in the Wellington area, Severn Valley Transport (this would go into liquidation in early 1931). Joseph Williamson continued in business at Shrewsbury and the trading-name was changed from Direct Motors to Williamson's Green Bus Service. The 'Maid of the Mountains' departed in 1929 when another (20-seat) Chevrolet arrived, and in 1930 the original 14-seat Chevrolet gave way to another example of the 20-seat variant. Chevrolets inevitably led to Bedfords, the first being a WLB delivered in October 1933, and for the remainder of the decade Mr Williamson see-sawed between vehicles of Bedford and Commer manufacture.

Two second-hand Commers arrived during the Second World War and the first of them was briefly replaced by a Dodge in 1947. All of the pre-war units had gone by 1950, thanks to a (relative) flood of new vehicles including three Bedford buses (one of them converted from a lorry chassis) and a Guy Vixen. The first Bedford SB, a Duple-bodied coach, arrived in September 1952 and brought the fleet to five.

No further fleet changes took place until 1961 when a second-hand SB replaced the Guy Vixen. This was also the year in which the founder passed control of the business to his son, CJ (John) Williamson. Bedfords continued to be favoured and in October 1970 the first 45-seat VAM arrived from Salopia of Whitchurch. More followed until 1979 when the company's allegiance shifted to Ford.

For 17 years from 1967 the stage-carriage services were operated by coaches, but in 1984 Williamson acquired a third-hand Leyland Leopard bus with high-density 63-seat Duple Dominant bodywork. This impressive machine continued as the principal vehicle on the local bus services during the deregulation period and well beyond. Several subsidised routes were acquired in the early 1990s, including a share in the 'Shrewsbury Park & Ride' services for which three low-floor Dennis Darts were acquired.

By 1993 the founder's grandson, Howard Williamson, was the sole proprietor. After five years at the helm he decided to relinquish the local bus services and sold these to Arriva Midlands

Longford bodywork was never common, and even less so on Bedford OB chassis, but Williamson of Shrewsbury ordered the combination in 1948 for this 28-seat bus. EUX 359 gave 17 years of service to the operator. (Malcolm Yeomans Collection)

In 1950 Williamson was persuaded to try a Guy Vixen bus and once again selected a rare bodybuilder, in this case Green. FNT 891, seen here in Shrewsbury on the Withington service, was traded in to the dealer Don Everall in the summer of 1961. (Chris Elmes Collection)

In exchange for the Vixen (and, presumably, some cash!) Williamson got MOD 688, a 1951 Bedford SB coach with Duple Vega bodywork licence-built by Brush. Everall had bought the vehicle from Midway of Crymmych. It was withdrawn from use in October 1970. (Author's Collection)

Mr John Williamson, son of the founder, stands in front of petrol-engined Bedford VAM3/Duple Viceroy coach HUX 244E, a 1967 vehicle bought from Salopia of Whitchurch to replace MOD 688. It retains Salopia livery with Williamsons Motorways titles. (Malcolm Knight)

North in August 1998. By the summer of 2000 the Williamson business had three vehicles left, all of them coaches, and went into liquidation in September of that year.

## Worthen of Brockton

In 1922 Mr Bernard Dillow Bunce of Worthen started a bus service between Shrewsbury and the Welsh town of Montgomery via his home village. The vehicle in use was registered NT 372 but its type remains unrecorded. On Mondays the service was extended to Welshpool for the market-day there, and despite competition from Midland Red Mr Bunce's enterprise, known as Worthen & District, prospered. By 1931 a Chevrolet and a new Bedford were maintaining the service, and after Midland Red withdrew from the Montgomery route in 1934 Mr Bunce responded by gradually enlarging his fleet. Between 1936 and 1942 he would buy no fewer than 12 Tilling-Stevens vehicles, seven of them formerly with Southdown.

Two Bedford OWB utility buses were delivered during the war, and in January 1943 the proprietor formed a limited company, Worthen & District Motor Services Ltd, to continue the business. However, in 1945 Mr Bunce decided to sell the company to the well-known Welsh independent Mid-Wales Motorways. It continued as a separate subsidiary of the Newtown firm until June 1958 although its vehicles were indistinguishable from those of the main fleet except by reading the 'legal lettering' on the nearside skirt panels.

In September 1963 the original Mid-Wales Motorways went into liquidation. A new version would emerge from the wreckage, but only after the receivers had sold off some parts of the old company's assets. The semi-autonomous unit at Worthen was an obvious candidate for disposal, and in October 1963 the Shrewsbury-Montgomery/Welshpool route and four vehicles (two Commer Avengers, a Crossley and a Bedford OB) were sold to Mr Thomas J Green of Brockton who had previously managed the Worthen depot for Mid-Wales. The vehicles' old MWM livery of blue and white was modified by over-painting the white areas with red, and the previously unofficial nickname of 'Worthen Motorways' was adopted as the trading name of the new enterprise. In April 1964 a fourth-hand Bedford SB/Duple coach was added to the fleet and this also received the blue/red livery, but all subsequent purchases were left in the colour schemes of their previous operators. These later arrivals included more SB coaches, a 44-seat AEC Reliance/Duple Midland service bus acquired from Jones of Aberbeeg in May 1966 and three Thames Trader coaches.

In September 1974 Mr Green (who had been suffering from ill health for some time) decided to retire and sold the business to a neighbouring independent operator, Valley of Bishops Castle (qv). Valley retained the Worthen garage as an out-station for the Montgomery route and acquired an additional service bus to cover the additional commitments. In later developments Valley would sell its Bishops Castle network to Minsterley (qv) in 1982 and the Worthen depot would become the company's main operational base. In May 1986, faced with the rigours of deregulation, Valley decided to get out of the bus and coach business and its remaining services and vehicles were sold to Mr David A Pye, trading as Worthen Travel. Mr Pye continued to operate the Montgomery/Welshpool routes into the 21st Century as Shropshire County Council services 558/559.

TJ Green acquired the Worthen-based operations of Mid-Wales in October 1963 and used the trading-name of Worthen Motorways. Commer Avenger I/Churchill coach CEP 168 was one of two which came with the business and was unusual in being fitted with a Bedford diesel engine in place of its original Commer petrol unit. As a result it lasted for three years longer than its Commer-powered 1951 contemporary, CEP 264, and was finally withdrawn in September 1968. (Brian Botley via Tim Butler)

Worthen Motorways' first 'proper' service bus was this 1957 AEC Reliance/Duple Midland, PNR 891, acquired from Jones of Aberbeeg in May 1966. It retained its original owner's livery and is seen here in Shrewsbury on the Montgomery service. (Geoff Mills)

# Part Three
# WELLINGTON AND TELFORD

The history of the area between Wellington and the Staffordshire boundary became irrevocably detached from that of the rest of Shropshire in 1709 when Abraham Darby migrated to the region from his native Bristol. Darby had worked in the malt industry and had realised that coke (the fuel used in the barley roasting ovens) could also be usefully employed to increase the temperature in iron-making furnaces, resulting in a purer and better product. By the time of his grandson the family's reputation was second to none, and in 1779 Abraham the Third demonstrated his inherited genius by building the Iron Bridge across the River Severn. It was the longest cast iron structure in the world and attracted substantial orders for the company's products.

Meanwhile a young Scottish stonemason, Thomas Telford, had moved to Shropshire in 1787, initially to build a rather grand house in Shrewsbury for a local Member of Parliament. His talents were swiftly recognised and in 1788 he was appointed as the county surveyor in charge of road construction and other large public projects. Telford's abilities were soon employed upon a wider stage. At the end of the 18th century he designed the cast iron trough for the 19-arch Pontcysyllte aqueduct which carried the Llangollen Canal across the River Dee in Denbighshire at a height of more than a hundred feet. His next project was even more ambitious; the construction of a modern highway from London to Holyhead for connections with ferry-boats bound for Dublin. The route followed the course of the old Roman road as far as the Shropshire/Denbighshire border and then veered westwards through difficult mountain terrain before reaching the Menai Strait between the Welsh mainland and the island of Anglesey. This notoriously turbulent tidal channel was crossed by Telford's crowning achievement, a magnificent suspension bridge completed in 1826.

When the British government decided to create a string of 'New Towns' in the early 1960s the majority of the chosen sites took their names from existing villages such as Milton Keynes, Peterlee, and Skelmersdale. The exception was the new community in central Shropshire which was originally known as Dawley New Town (after one of the largest villages in the area) but was swiftly re-named to honour the Scottish immigrant who had done so much to improve the county's transportation system. The new community's location astride Telford's super-highway to Holyhead made the choice an appropriate one.

## The SOA 'Rotas'

The Mid-Shropshire Omnibus Association was founded in 1928, to represent the interests of the small bus operators in the Wellington area and to establish an equitable 'rota' system on the two main service corridors to Donnington and Oakengates. This rationalisation was made necessary by the fact that there were 14 operators on the former route and no fewer than 16 on the latter, not counting Midland Red. A third 'rota' governed the seasonal routes from the Wellington area to The Wrekin, a local hill which attracted sightseers from far and wide.

When the 1930 Road Traffic Act abolished the licensing powers of local authorities and established regional Traffic Commissioners in their stead, the Wellington area operators feared that they would be excluded from the process. In 1931 they shortened the name of their organisation to the Shropshire Omnibus Association (which was less accurate but sounded more impressive) and decided to apply for licences collectively under the SOA name. It was also agreed that the revamped Association would give its members 'first refusal' rights when any other member decided to sell their business, effectively preventing any further expansion in the area by Midland Red. The Birmingham-based company saw these manoeuvres as a restraint of trade and made strenuous objections to the authorities. As a result, in 1933, the Traffic Commissioners reversed their original ruling and demanded that all licences should be held by individual operators rather than by the SOA. It was a minor victory for Midland Red as all of its other objections were dismissed as unfounded.

In 1951, belatedly recognising that the SOA could not be beaten, Midland Red agreed to co-ordinate its Donnington and Oakengates services with those of the local operators and to publish a joint timetable for the area. At around the same time route numbers began to appear on the SOA members' vehicles, or at least on those which had the capability to display them. The 'Oakengates rota' services became Nos 1-6 to denote the different routings between Wellington and Oakengates, and the various ultimate destinations including Lamb Corner, Priors Lee and St Georges. The 'Donnington rota' services were similarly numbered from 20-24, although in this case the route designator gave little clue as to the final destination at the Donnington end (which could be Bell Gate, the Coal Wharf or the Roundabout, with certain journeys opting for Humbers or Muxton Corner). Another two decades would pass before the balance of power started to shift from the independents to BMMO and standardised poppy red Leyland Nationals would begin to replace the multicoloured fleets of the SOA.

## Archway of Shifnal

Compared to the other operators featured in this book, Archway Motors of Shifnal was a newcomer. Founded in June 1968 by Arthur H Evans and TR Wood, the company made its living from a typical mixture of private-hire and contract work for the first five years of its existence, using several 'pre-owned' vehicles.

In December 1972 Mr Evans became the sole proprietor and twelve months later Archway started its first two stage-carriage services. One, a Friday/Saturday run from Shifnal to the recently opened shopping complex at Telford Town Centre, was entirely new. The other, a Wednesday/Saturday service from Sheriffhales and Shifnal to Bridgnorth, was a truncated version of a route discarded by the Staffordshire operator Happy Days. To operate these services Archway acquired a Weymann -odied Tiger Cub bus which had been new to North Western but came from Silcox of Pembroke Dock. Further 'niche' services for shoppers and other consumers followed, and a second Tiger Cub bus (new to Yorkshire Woollen) was acquired in 1979 from neighbouring operator Elcock of Ironbridge. The two Tiger Cubs were given the names 'The Shifnal Flyer' and 'The Shifnal Express'.

In the early 1980s the Tiger Cubs were replaced by 36-feet long vehicles including four BET-style Leopards (new to Trent and Southdown) and – far more surprisingly – three

Leyland Tiger Cub/Weymann Hermes service bus KDB 647 was new to North Western in 1956, passing to Silcox of Pembroke Dock in January 1969. Silcox sold it to Archway Motors of Shifnal in October 1973. Iits new name ('The Shifnal Flyer') was presumably a reference to the Wright Brothers. (Chris Warn Collection)

Despite the registration GUY 768 this is not an Arab III but a Daimler CVD6 with 33-seat Burlingham coach bodywork. New in 1948 it came to Ashley of Dawley in November 1961 and gave two years of service to them before being scrapped. (Peter Harden Collection)

Ashley of Dawley bought this 1948 Daimler CVD6/Willowbrook bus, LTN 470, from Newcastle Corporation in May 1957. Seen here passing Midland Red's Wellington offices, it was withdrawn from service in late 1960 and scrapped. (Roy Marshall via B Mel Gough)

BMMO built S23s, a type rarely seen outside of the Midland Red or (latterly) West Midlands PTE fleets. The Archway examples came from the PTE and were thus conveniently painted in blue and cream, an approximation of their new owner's existing colour scheme. Many other second-hand purchases were operated in the remains of their previous owners' liveries (regardless of colour) or in bland overall white without any titles beyond their legal lettering.

Archway 'grew like Topsy' after deregulation, operating both commercial and tendered services in the Telford area, and soon became an attractive proposition as a take-over target. In 1989 it was acquired by the Shearings group which had already acquired Salopia (qv) in the north of Shropshire. As a direct consequence Shearings closed its (ex-Salopia) regional headquarters in Whitchurch and moved its focus of operations in the county to Shifnal. In 1992 the Shearings group's bus interests were sold to a management and employee buy-out team and became known as Timeline Travel, and in 1998 Timeline itself was swallowed up by Midland Red North (soon to become Arriva Midlands North).

## Ashley of Dawley

Before the development of Telford New Town and (ten years later) its Town Centre retail complex, the traditional shopping venues for inhabitants of the industrial villages in the area to the east of Wellington were found in Wellington itself, Dawley and Oakengates. A route between Wellington and Dawley was thus an attractive one in terms of passenger flow, even more so if slightly diverted to serve the large village of Ketley along the way.

In 1947 this important daily service passed from GA Darrall of Dawley (trading as Supreme Motor Services) to William Smith of Donnington Wood (qv). A more modest (Thursday only) link between the two towns was provided by William Hart of Dawley with two small 'bonneted Bedford' coaches, Hart's service taking a more direct but less well-populated route through the village of Lawley. Mr Hart decided to sell the business in September 1951 and it passed to JD (Jack) Ashley, although the vendor retained his title to the Bedfords until June 1952. Ashley bought a third vehicle shortly afterwards, a 1938 Dodge with 27-seat bus bodywork by Grose, and

then a fourth in the same year, a Bedford OB with highly unusual (some would say grotesque) coach bodywork manufactured by Willenhall.

William Smith died in 1953 and his company was subsequently divided into three parts by his four sons. In 1954, possibly to offset the death duties on their father's estate, the Smith brothers decided to sell the profitable Dawley to Wellington route before selecting their own portions of the remaining assets. The buyer was Jack Ashley who vastly increased his stage-carriage work as a result. Larger vehicles (all of them second-hand or worse) began to appear, including 33-seat Maudslay Marathon and Guy Arab coaches and a 35-seat Daimler CVD6 bus which replaced the odd-looking OB/Willenhall in June 1958. Ironically, this monstrosity was sold to George P Smith, one of the sons of William.

Jack Ashley died prematurely in 1960 and control of the business passed to JD Ashley Jr. The first pair of many Bedford SB coaches arrived in the summer of 1960, and in March 1961 were followed by two more Daimler CVD6s. One had a 33-seat Willenhall coach body of reasonably attractive proportions (at least when compared to the notorious OB) while the other was a bus version which had been new to an Isle of Wight operator but arrived in Dawley from Hampson of Oswestry.

In 1963 the founder's widow Kathleen became the company's proprietor (in place of her son) and her first acquisition was a particularly unusual vehicle, an underfloor-engined Daimler Freeline with Alexander bus bodywork. New to Glasgow Corporation in 1953, its central entrance and lack of seats (36 instead of the normal 44) betrayed it as a 'standee' vehicle, or 'crush-loader' as they were more pejoratively known. It was evident that Mrs Ashley considered it less than ideal as it was sold after 18 months at Dawley and replaced by a Bedford SB/Duple Midland bus. This was itself replaced in January 1969 by a newer SB bus with (rare in civilian guise) Strachan Pacesaver bodywork.

The first Bedford VAM coach was acquired in early 1971 and was followed by a Duple Midland -bodied bus version which had been new to Victoria Motorways of Woodville in Derbyshire. In 1973 JD Ashley Jr returned to the proprietorship in succession to his mother, and five years later he sold the stage-carriage operations to Midland

The 1951 registration of Ashley's NAU 900 didn't tell the whole story as its post-war Strachan coach body was mounted on a refurbished 1932 vintage AEC Regent double-deck chassis which had been new to Nottingham as TV 6750. Ashley acquired it from a Herefordshire operator in August 1957 and sold it to Churchbridge of Cannock three years later. Also visible in this magnificent scene are Ashley's Marathon II/Duple coach EAY 985 and Hoggins' OB/Mulliner bus GAW 759. (Roy Marshall via B Mel Gough)

Impressed by earlier Daimler service buses, Mrs Ashley decided to try an underfloor-engined Daimler Freeline. Alexander-bodied 'standee' vehicle FYS 521, new in 1953, arrived from Glasgow Corporation in September 1963 but had been sold for scrap by April 1965. (Roy Marshall via B Mel Gough)

The Freeline was replaced by a second-hand Bedford SB/Duple Midland bus, and in January 1969 that vehicle was traded in for a newer model. GTG 152C had been delivered new to Bebb of Llantwit Fardre in 1965 and was an SB5 with 'Ministry style' Strachan Pacesaver bodywork. (Author's Collection)

The Pacesaver gave way in its turn to this Bedford VAM5/Duple Midland service bus, HFA 208E, which had been new to Victoria Motorways of Woodville in 1967. It is seen on Ashley's main stage-carriage service after its diversion into the site of Telford's 'Town Centre' development. (Roy Marshall via B Mel Gough)

CRW 327 was one of a batch of Dennis Lancet 2s with Willowbrook dual-purpose bodywork built for the coach operator Bunty of Coventry in 1937. In mid-1942 it passed to AT Brown of Trench and is seen here in Donnington on a 'rota' timing. After 17 years with Brown it was sold to Hoggins of Wrockwardine Wood for further service. (Roy Marshall via B Mel Gough)

The venerable Lancet's replacement was VDA 32, the 1958 Guy Warrior WU/Willowbrook service bus demonstrator. Despite an extensive sales tour it failed to attract a single order and was acquired by AT Brown in January 1959. Whilst not quite as long-lived as its predecessor, it did last into the early 1970s. (Geoff Mills)

Red. The Ashley family's services were never involved in the SOA 'rotas' but passed into the NBC subsidiary's ownership on the same day, 1st April 1978.

The coaching side of the business continued until December 1981 when it was sold to a neighbouring operator, Elcock of Ironbridge, and by the end of 1982 all of the vehicles had been repainted into Elcock livery and the Ashley name had disappeared. Mr Ashley himself became an Elcock employee for several years until his retirement.

# AT Brown of Trench

Alfred T Brown opened a service from his home village of Trench to Wellington in 1926 using a 14-seat Chevrolet, and his company remained loyal to the brand (in its Chevrolet, GMC, and Bedford manifestations) for more than sixty years. The original route had become an SOA 'Donnington rota' service by 1931, and by 1938 was being operated by a Bedford WTL (with 20-seat bus bodywork assembled by Brown himself to a Thurgood design) and a 25-seat WTB bus with Duple bodywork.

The outbreak of war in September 1939 resulted in an increasing demand from soldiers at the Donnington Garrison and workers at the Central Ordnance Depot, and in 1942 a 39-seat Dennis Lancet 2 was acquired from a Coventry operator. Soon afterwards the two pre-war Bedfords were further supplemented by the delivery of two 32-seat OWB utility buses. These were predictably unpopular with passengers accustomed to more comfortable conveyances and were sold off fairly rapidly after the end of the conflict, unlike the Lancet 2 which lasted until July 1959 and then passed to Hoggins of Wrockwardine Wood (qv) for a few more years of service to the local residents.

Until 1947 all vehicles had been configured for stage-carriage work but in the post-war era the company began to look further afield for its revenues. A seasonal express service was inaugurated from Trench to Llandudno, and a second route from Donnington to Llandudno was acquired from FH Davies of Snedshill. A third service from the area to the Welsh resort was operated by Lowe of Hadley (qv) and by 1948 Brown and Lowe were jointly marketing their operations as the 'North Wales Express Service'.

Brown's contribution to these schedules was provided by several brand-new vehicles including three Bedford OB/Duple Vistas, a Duple-bodied Dennis Lancet J3,and a Crossley SD42 with Burlingham bodywork, all in Brown's two-tone green and cream livery which contrasted nicely with the red and cream colour scheme used by Lowe. The first Bedford SB coach arrived in 1951 and would be followed by later variants of the same breed until the mid-1960s.

In 1953 a neighbouring 'Donnington rota' operator, Frederick Priest of Trench, passed away and his timings were added to those already operated by AT Brown. An additional coaching commitment came in the same year when the company started a 'Forces Leave' military express service from Donnington to Birmingham. This lasted until 1963 when the local Garrison was severely diminished in importance by cuts in defence spending.

The pre-war Lancet 2 continued as the main vehicle on the 'rota' service until 1959 when it was replaced by an underfloor-engined Guy Warrior with Willowbrook bus bodywork. A former demonstrator which attracted few (if any) orders, the vehicle nevertheless gave good service to Brown and remained in use until the 1970s.

In 1962 Mr WHW Lowe of Hadley decided to retire from the bus industry. His 'rota' timings passed to Smiths Eagle (qv) but the express service to Llandudno was absorbed into those of AT Brown, and in May 1963 a limited company, AT Brown (Coaches) Ltd, was created to supersede the now redundant 'North Wales Express Service' consortium. This entity also became the licence holder for the 'rota' operation in the following year.

The first Bedford VAM, a second-hand 45-seat Duple-bodied coach, arrived in March 1968 and most of Brown's coaches from this time onwards were acquired from other operators while still relatively new. By 1978 the company's assorted coaching activities were producing far more revenue than its stage-carriage service and the company was among the majority of SOA members who voted to sell the 'rota' operations to Midland Red. The business retained its Llandudno express services and other coaching work, and by the 1990s the fleet of Bedfords was being gradually replaced by newer vehicles of DAF and Dennis manufacture.

The collapse of a neighbouring operator, Britannia Travel, in 2004 brought an increase in schools contracts, works services and private-hire commitments and the coach fleet grew from 10 to 15 as a result. The company also briefly re-entered the local bus service market in 2003-05 as the successful bidder for a tendered route between Market Drayton and Whitchurch. AT Brown (Coaches) Ltd remains in business as one of the leading coach operators in the Telford area, and in 2009 one of its vehicles featured in a James May television programme, transporting schoolchildren to RAF Cosford to assemble a life-size 'Airfix' Spitfire model.

# H Brown of Donnington Wood

Harry A Brown was one of the earliest bus operators in the Wellington area, commencing a regular service from Donnington Wood to the market town in 1920 with an eight-seat Daimler motor-car. A 14-seat Ford Model T char-a-banc followed, pursued by three 14-seat Chevrolets, and in 1926 Harry Brown opened a second route from the Donnington area to Oakengates. Vehicles with a larger capacity were soon needed and in 1929 a 20-seat GMC was delivered.

The original route (soon to be absorbed into the SOA's 'Donnington rota' system) and the Donnington to Oakengates route (which remained independent of SOA supervision) were joined in the late 1920s by new market-day only services to Market Drayton (on Wednesdays) and Childs Ercall (on Fridays). The Oakengates service was itself extended during the 1930s with some timings continuing to Humbers and Muxton Corner at the northern end, and to Ketley at the southern end, while the frequency of the route was increased to meet the growing military demand for capacity between Donnington Garrison and Oakengates railway station.

Vehicle acquisitions during the 1930s included two 20-seat Commers, two more second-hand GMCs, two new Leyland coaches (a Cub and a Tiger), a new Bedford WTB coach delivered in 1937 and a second-hand 32-seat Dennis Lancet. By 1937 two of Mr Brown's brothers had joined the business as partners along with his four sons; Clifford, Percy, Sidney and Alfred (the latter not to be confused with Alfred T Brown of Trench) and the business thus continued after the founder's death, at a relatively early age, in 1938.

Strangely perhaps, given the numerous military and industrial facilities on the operator's doorstep, no new Bedford OWB utility buses were allocated to the company during the Second World War. Delivered in their stead were a variety of second-hand vehicles including six additional pre-war Lancets and two more Bedford WTBs. A fourth WTB was acquired with the business of W Evans of Wrockwardine Wood, purchased in 1942. The Browns finally got their solitary Bedford OWB two years after the war ended, a second-hand example bought to replace the surviving pre-war GMC.

The remaining pre-war stock was eliminated between 1947 and 1951 by an impressive number of brand-new vehicles including two Dennis Lancet J3s, two Crossleys, three (rare) Vulcan 6PF buses and – most famously – five Sentinel SLC4/35 coaches. From the time of their arrival the Sentinels were used on the stage-carriage services as well as on coaching work and Browns would boast repeatedly of their 'locally made buses' for the next two decades. Two more Sentinels, another SLC4/35 coach and an STC4/40 bus, would join the fleet in April 1953. Both were former demonstrators made redundant by the deletion of the models which they represented from the Sentinel catalogue.

The additional vehicles were made necessary by the acquisition of licences for 'Forces Leave' express services from the Donnington army camp to Birmingham, London and Manchester during 1953. These would continue until the facility's virtual closure ten years later and provided a valuable source of income to an operator with no seasonal express services to seaside resorts. Another vehicle which became a regular performer on these military services was an intriguing hybrid, a pre-war AEC Regal chassis which received a post-war coach body by WS Yeates, and was then re-registered to reflect its 'mutton dressed as lamb' status.

After this massive spending spree no further vehicles would be purchased until 1959 when a second STC4/40 bus was acquired from Warner of Tewkesbury. The vehicle had originally been a Sentinel demonstrator and had also seen service with a London coach operator. It was followed in the same year by two new Bedford SB/Duple coaches and five more of these arrived in 1962-65. As a result of this influx of modernity the Sentinel SLC4/35s were no longer required for coaching

Vulcan had been acquired by Tilling-Stevens before the war, but in the late 1940s the name was briefly revived for the 6PF lightweight goods and passenger models. Most of the latter carried Dutfield bodywork including a batch of three 32-seat buses delivered to H Brown of Donnington Wood in 1949. This one is FUJ 19 which ran for Browns until August 1959. None of the three saw further PSV service. (Roy Marshall via B Mel Gough)

Nice as the Vulcans were, the Browns were even more well-known for their fleet of Sentinels. Beadle-bodied SLC4/35 coach HAW 374, new in 1951, was the only one (of the five delivered that year) which would keep its original centre entrance configuration throughout its working life. The vehicle remained active until February 1970. (Geoff Mills)

While HAW 374 kept hold of its central entrance until the very end, the Browns' other SLC4/35s were converted to front entrance and fitted with 41 bus seats between 1965 and 1969. HNT 49 was thus modified in 1966 and is currently preserved at a site in Herefordshire. (Geoff Mills)

The Browns' fleet was a treasure-trove of oddities. This is JUX 550, which had a secret. Its pre-war AEC Regal chassis had been new to City Of Oxford as BFC 38, originally fitted with a Park Royal bus body. The Browns acquired it from a travelling showman in 1953, scrapped the dilapidated bodywork, and replaced it with a Yeates coach body transferred from another vehicle. The body-swap was carried out by Metalcraft of Blythe Bridge which added the full-front as shown. In this form, and suitably re-registered, it ran until August 1960. (Roy Marshall via B Mel Gough)

duties, and most were converted into one-man-operated buses by moving their entrances from the centre to the front and equipping them with 41 bus seats in place of their 35 coach seats. Browns performed these conversions 'in house' with commendable skill.

In 1967 the company successfully applied for its first 'civilian' express routes, seasonal services to Bournemouth, Margate and Southsea on the English Channel coast. These were operated by the SB/Duple fleet alongside two larger Bedfords, a 52-seat VAL and a 45-seat VAM, purchased new in 1965/66. Meanwhile, the aging Sentinels had become something of a tourist attraction in their own right and led many transport enthusiasts to visit the Telford area in the late 1960s and early 1970s. Fears that they might disappear abruptly after the introduction of the government's 'Bus Grant' scheme in 1968 proved groundless, but in 1971 the rate of this subsidy was increased from 25% to 50% and Browns could no longer resist the temptation. Two new Bedford YRQ/ Willowbrook buses arrived in that year and the three most decrepit Sentinels were withdrawn from use. The remaining five managed to cling on until 1973, with the oldest having given more than 22 years of service. No fewer than four of Browns' eight Sentinels are still in existence, including an STC4/40 bus (to be found in the Aston Manor museum in Birmingham) and three SLC4/35s which are currently stored at a site in Herefordshire by Mr David Wheatley.

While the age of the Sentinel at Browns had been a long one, the age of the Bedford/ Willowbrook bus would prove to be short-lived. After a vote by SOA members it was agreed that the 'rota' services would pass to Midland Red on 1st April 1978. In addition (via a separate negotiation) Browns' other stage services also passed to the NBC subsidiary on the same date.

The remainder of the Browns business, including the seasonal express services, was transferred to a new consortium known briefly as BMB Operators. The initials stood for Browns, Martlew and Britannia, and after two months the partners in this consortium acquired Wrekin Coach Services Ltd from its original owners (another grouping of Telford area operators) and reversed their own syndicate into the limited company. WCS then adopted the trading-name of Britannia Travel which had previously been the

brand-name used by Gerald E Smith. The further history of this operator can be found under the heading of 'William Smith & Successors' later in this chapter.

# Cooper of Oakengates

At an undetermined point in the mid-1920s Mr RG (George) Cooper, then resident in the village of Wrockwardine Wood, started a bus service from Oakengates to Wellington via Ketley. By 1927 three 14-seat Willys-Overland vehicles were in use and were followed by two 20-seat GMC buses in 1929/31. Membership of the SOA led to a share of the 'Oakengates rota' schedule, and in 1934 the share of this service previously operated by Abraham Taylor was divided between Cooper and Hoggins of Wrockwardine Wood (qv). The Cooper fleet continued to grow and 1936 deliveries included a five-year old Dodge (a 26-seat bus) and a brand-new Bedford WTB coach. Four more factory-fresh WTBs would arrive in 1937-39.

Expansion outside of the Wellington area took place in April 1938 when Cooper acquired the business of R Jones & Company of Shrewsbury. The purchase included three vehicles (a Chevrolet, a Reo and a Vulcan) and stage-carriage services from Shrewsbury westwards to Four Crosses and Welshpool. These proved difficult to administer from a distance and in September 1939 were sold to Mid-Wales Motorways at a considerable profit – MWM was particularly anxious to cross the border and to connect their rural route network to that of Midland Red at Shrewsbury.

Wartime deliveries to Cooper (by then removed from Wrockwardine Wood to larger premises in Oakengates) included four OWB utility buses and a pre-war assortment of another GMC, a Gilford, a Dennis Lancet and (most unusually of all) a Sentinel-HSG with 32-seat Cowieson bus bodywork. This former demonstrator, which had originally been fuelled by a producer-gas unit, was quickly converted into a more orthodox bus by the removal of the HSG ('High Speed Gas') equipment, the installation of a petrol tank and the restoration of its Hercules engine to standard configuration. Withdrawn in the 1950s, this unique vehicle became seriously derelict at the Oakengates premises but was later rescued for preservation. After many years in storage with various owners in the north-east of England and at

Cooper of Oakengates acquired a large fleet of Crossleys in 1948-50. Most were coaches but there were also two Burlingham-bodied buses. EUX 182 was delivered in November 1948 and was sold to a Wolverhampton contractor in October 1959. (Roy Marshall via B Mel Gough)

This Crossley SD42 with Burlingham coach bodywork was acquired second-hand in March 1955. EUX 321, new in 1949, came to Cooper from Fisher of Bronington and remained in service until December 1963. Like many of the Crossleys it was scrapped at Ketley Steel Works. (Roy Marshall via B Mel Gough)

Cooper's most famous Crossleys were the five delivered in 1948/49 with fully-fronted coach bodywork by Junction Coachcraft of Manchester. EUX 74, seen here in its original condition, was later rebodied with the half-cab Metalcraft unit from Crossley GAW 380. It was withdrawn in January 1964. (Roy Marshall via B Mel Gough)

There was also a solitary Tilling-Stevens with identical Junction bodywork, FAW 923, delivered to Cooper in June 1949. Withdrawn after ten years in service, it found no buyer and was scrapped. (Roy Marshall via B Mel Gough)

Cooper also tried an Austin CXB amid the massed deliveries of Crossleys. FAW 547 had 26-seat coach bodywork by Strachan and was delivered in April 1949. Withdrawn from use in October 1960, it went for scrap. (Roy Marshall via B Mel Gough)

There was a gap between the departure of the last half-cab bus (a Burlingham-bodied Crossley) in April 1965 and the arrival of the next generation of service buses, a pair of Bedford VAM5s with Duple Midland bodywork, in January 1966. This one is FAW 156D. (Geoff Mills)

the Scottish Vintage Bus Museum in Fife, it was offered for sale again in late 2009.

The four OWBs apparently made a favourable impression upon George Cooper as immediate post-war deliveries included 15 brand-new Bedford OBs (five of them in bus configuration) which replaced most of the pre-war stock. Other acquisitions included two 33-seat Maudslay Marathon coaches in 1948, and single examples of the Commer Q4 and Austin CXB in 1949, but these were soon to be overshadowed by another large order for new chassis. This resulted in the arrival of 14 Crossley SD42s in 1949/50 which replaced almost the entire fleet. Two of the 1949 Crossleys were 35-seat Burlingham-bodied buses, one a 33-seat Burlingham coach, two had coach bodywork by Metalcraft, and the remaining five had attractive fully-fronted coach bodywork by Junction Coachcraft of Manchester. An identical Junction body was fitted to a single Tilling-Stevens delivered in June 1949. The balance of the Crossley order, delivered in 1950 carried Metalcraft half-cab bodywork and these were followed by a 40-seat Sentinel STC4/40 bus in August of the same year.

The company had originally ordered two STC4/40s but the first proved troublesome and was returned to the manufacturer after less than two years in service. The order for the second machine was cancelled as a result of these difficulties and it became a Sentinel demonstrator in full Cooper livery (including titles), erroneously suggesting an element of customer satisfaction which was far from the truth. In 1951 it visited several operators, including PMT, but attracted no orders before being sold off to a Yorkshire company in early 1952.

Cooper continued to increase his share of the traffic on the main Oakengates-Wellington corridor, acquiring the 'rota' operations of FH Davies of Snedshill in April 1949, J & W Jackson of Oakengates in October 1950, and Joseph Guy of Ketley Bank in June 1951. Later in that year George Cooper's son, Douglas, became a full partner in the business, and would be joined by other members of the family as time progressed. An underfloor-engined AEC Regal IV coach with Duple bodywork was tried in 1952, but all subsequent deliveries of new coaches would be of Bedford manufacture, including SBs, VALs and VAMs. The stage-carriage services became the

preserve of the Crossley fleet until the mid-1960s, with the Metalcraft-bodied examples lasting longer than the stylish but structurally weaker Junction-bodied vehicles.

An unexpected period of expansion began in 1962 when the Coopers acquired the 'Oakengates rota' shares of Hoggins of Wrockwardine Wood and Edward D Smith of Trench. Both of these operators continued to trade, but in July 1964 the Cooper partnership acquired the entire business of Jervis of Wellington (qv) along with three vehicles (a fully-fronted AEC Regal III coach, a bus-bodied Leyland Tiger half-cab, and an all-Leyland Royal Tiger coach) and yet another share of the 'Oakengates rota'. These purchases made Coopers by far the most important operator on the Oakengates-Wellington corridor as the holder of four sevenths of the surviving shares in the route. The company was also becoming a major player in the local coaching arena. In 1966 the Coopers joined forces with Elcock of Ironbridge, Hoggins of Wrockwardine Wood and Smiths Eagle of Trench in the formation of Wrekin Coach Services Ltd. This jointly owned enterprise operated no vehicles of its own but served as a centralised booking agency for the seasonal expresses, excursions, tours and private-hire activities of its four shareholders.

The first new buses in more than 15 years arrived in early 1966 in the shape of two Bedford VAMs with Willowbrook bodywork and these were followed by a similarly bodied YRQ model in March 1971. These belated replacements for the time-expired Crossleys were destined to be among Coopers' final vehicles. In 1973 the company broke ranks with the rest of the SOA and on 15th November the entire business was sold to Midland Red, an act seen as an outright betrayal by some of the other SOA proprietors. Wrekin Coach Services Ltd remained in existence as an instrumentality of its three surviving shareholders, but the SOA had lost its largest and most influential member and things would never be quite the same again.

# Excelsior of Wrockwardine Wood

In 1924 Alfred Price of Wrockwardine Wood (proprietor of the Excelsior Garage) bought a Ford Model T hearse, converted it to carry the living, and began to offer excursions and private-hire services to his customers. By 1926 this

Excelsior of Wrockwardine Wood bought this 1949 Bedford OB/Mulliner bus, JRT 41, in August 1958 and used it on the 'rota' service until May 1963. After withdrawal it became a mobile shop in Coleshill. (Roy Marshall via B Mel Gough)

The replacement for JRT 41 was 1951 Bedford SB/Duple Vega coach KWX 413, acquired from the Sheffield-area operator Wigmore of Dinnington in June 1963. In July 1965 Excelsior sold it to Canham of Whittlesey but the vehicle would return to Shropshire two years later with Williamson of Shrewsbury. (Author's Collection)

Excelsior's first purpose-built service bus for several years arrived in July 1969 in the shape of VAM5/Duple Midland HCJ 800D. New to Yeomans of Canon Pyon in 1966, it stayed with Excelsior until 1972 when it was sold to Eaglen of Gainsborough. (Roy Marshall via B Mel Gough)

Unlike most of the SOA operators, Excelsior continued to provide local bus services after the 1st of April 1978. This impressive new Leyland Leopard with 63-seat Duple Dominant bus bodywork, BAW 1T, arrived in the following year. After Excelsior's demise it passed briefly to Elcock and then to Williamson of Shrewsbury. (Roy Marshall via B Mel Gough)

vehicle had been replaced by a 14-seat Chevrolet and Price was operating timetabled departures on a route from the Oakengates area to Wellington. This service would become part of the SOA's 'Oakengates rota' in 1931. A second Chevrolet, a 14-seat char-a-banc, had been acquired in 1927 but replaced two years later by a 20-seat Star bus, and in 1936 the Star was traded in for a Bedford WTB coach which would become Excelsior's solitary vehicle during the Second World War.

Expansion in earnest came in 1946 when the WTB was joined by a second Bedford coach, a brand-new OB/Duple Vista. In May 1948 the fleet grew to four by the addition of new examples of the Guy Arab III (with a Santus coach body) and Tilling-Stevens K-series (with coach bodywork by Dutfield). A second OB replaced the 1946 machine in 1950, maintaining the fleet's low age-profile despite the 1936 vintage WTB (which survived until 1956). The remainder of the decade witnessed the purchase of three Bedford SB/Duple coaches (two new, one used) and three more OBs (two buses in their turn and a coach which finally replaced the WTB).

The founder was at first joined and then succeeded by his son, Reginald A Price. Under his direction all purchases after 1960 were of Bedfords except for an (ex-East Midland) 35-seat AEC Regal II/Willowbrook bus operated for a year from February 1962. The last of the two OB buses was withdrawn from use in May 1963 and for the next six years the 'rota' operation would be maintained by SB coaches. Excelsior also purchased two 52-seat VAL coaches and several VAMs, including one with 45-seat dual-purpose bodywork by Duple Midland which arrived in July 1969. This became the regular vehicle on the 'Oakengates rota' workings, a commitment which increased in April 1973 when Priory of Priors Lee (qv) closed down and its 'rota' timings were taken over by Excelsior.

When the SOA voted to sell its members' 'rota' services to Midland Red with effect from 1st April 1978, Reg Price provided a dissenting voice. He refused to be bowed by the majority decision (the licence was, after all, in his own name) and vowed to continue. This was awkward for Midland Red as the NBC company had already planned its schedules and vehicle allocations in the expectation of a unanimous sell-out. Their solution was to offer Excelsior a route-swap in order to get rid of

them. Mr Price accepted Midland Red's hourly Wellington to Muxton Corner service in exchange for his original route and also acquired a works service from Wellington to Granville Colliery as a deal-clincher.

In 1979 a new stage-carriage vehicle arrived in the shape of a 63-seat ('maximum density') Leyland Leopard/Duple Dominant bus. The ten 'extra' seats were crammed into the vehicle by using three-plus-two seating on most rows, making it profoundly uncomfortable for all but the skinniest of customers on all but the shortest of rides. On the other hand it avoided the need for passengers to stand on busy journeys, and such vehicles were briefly popular (although mainly with operators of schools services).

The partnership of Reg Price and his wife Mildred gave way to a limited company, Excelsior Coachways (Telford) Ltd, in March 1983. Exactly two years later Excelsior ceased to trade and many of its assets (including the Leopard bus) were acquired by Elcock of Madeley, a long-established coach firm which had previously been based in Ironbridge. Mr and Mrs Price had already founded a new coach company of their own before the Excelsior closure, but the history of this later enterprise (known as Solitaire) is beyond the scope of this book.

# Hoggins of Wrockwardine Wood

The Hoggins story, as with so many other tales of independent bus operators, began with a Ford Model T. In 1921 William R Hoggins acquired one for private-hire work, and in 1924 used it to commence daily services from his home village of Wrockwardine Wood to Wellington via Oakengates and Hadley and from Oakengates to Wellington via Ketley Bank. The next recorded vehicles after the Ford were a 14-seat Willys-Overland bus in 1926, a 14-seat Chevrolet coach in 1927 and a 20-seat GMC bus in 1929 which replaced the 1927 Chevrolet. These were all delivered 'new', as was a 20-seat Thornycroft coach acquired in 1930.

In 1931 Hoggins' main services were incorporated into the SOA's 'Oakengates rota' and in 1934 the operator's first Bedford was delivered, a 20-seat WLB bus. Another would arrive in 1935, shortly before the founder went into partnership with his son, Thomas, as WR Hoggins & Son. In June 1937 a new 25-seat Leyland Cub bus replaced the first of the WLBs, while in 1938/39 second-hand examples of the Chevrolet and Bedford marques joined the fleet to cater for the increasing demand from local industry, revitalised by the inevitable rearmament process occasioned by German militarism.

The same demand justified the allocation of two Bedford OWB utility buses in 1942/44, but after the end of the war these vehicles were rapidly sold off and replaced by two bus-bodied OBs with more comfortable interiors. The first of three new Harrington-bodied Commer Commando coaches also joined the fleet in 1947 and over the next few years the Commers rubbed shoulders with further OBs (both new and second-hand), two pre-war WTBs and a pair of pre-war Dennis Lancet 39-seaters. The Bedford SB was a surprisingly late arrival in the Hoggins coach fleet (marketed in post-war years as 'Pilot Coaches') with the first being purchased in October 1954 to replace a smaller OB. The larger vehicle was needed to operate a new 'Forces Leave' military express service from the Donnington army camp to Liverpool.

In 1955 the founder died and Thomas Hoggins became the sole proprietor until the business passed to a partnership of Thomas, his wife and their two sons Donald and David in 1959. One factor involved in the timing of this change was a major expansion of the company's operations. In March 1959 the Hoggins family acquired the business of William Smith & Sons (qv) of Donnington Wood along with three vehicles (two of which had gone by the end of the year) and an important 'non-rota' service from Oakengates to Dawley via Ketley Bank.

A rather 'retro' acquisition in July 1959 was a 39-seat pre-war Dennis Lancet 2, previously operated by AT Brown of Trench. It lasted until June 1962 (when it was 25 years old) and was joined in 1959/60 by two post-war Lancet J3 coaches, briefly used as 'duplicates' on the stage-carriage services. Arrivals in 1961 were a third-hand Crossley coach with Duple bodywork and a relatively rare Morris Commercial OPR with 31-seat coach bodywork by Plaxton. The latter machine looked particularly smart in Hoggins' black and white livery with the 'Pilot Coaches' fleetname, and became the target of many an enthusiast's camera lens during its three year stay with the operator.

The 'Forces Leave' express to Liverpool came to an end for lack of traffic in 1961, and in 1962 the Hoggins family decided to reduce their commitment to stage-carriage work. The two 'rota' services in the Oakengates to Wellington corridor were sold to Cooper of Oakengates (qv), leaving Hoggins with the daily Oakengates to Dawley route recently acquired from William Smith & Sons and an assortment of works and hospital services. In the aftermath of this radical down-sizing the Dawley service was usually operated by the Morris Commercial and a bus-bodied OB until the arrival of a brand-new Bedford SB5/Duple Midland bus in September 1963.

In 1966 Hoggins became a participant in the Wrekin Coach Services Ltd consortium alongside Cooper of Oakengates, Elcock of Ironbridge and Smiths Eagle of Trench. As noted in the Cooper entry, this was a non-operational booking agency and Hoggins' contribution to the pool included a licence for excursions and tours from Wrockwardine Wood and the use of its coaching fleet of three SBs and a 52-seat VAL. A second-hand Thames Trader with Duple bodywork joined this quartet before the end of the year and was the first Ford product to enter the fleet since the original Model T in 1921. It was followed by two second-hand Bedford VAMs and then by another Ford, a new R192 coach with Duple bodywork which arrived in 1968. In 1972 a new Ford R192 bus with 47-seat Plaxton Derwent bodywork was delivered and became the front-line vehicle on the stage service, partially replacing the 1963 Bedford SB5.

A Ford had been Hoggins' first bus and the R192/Derwent would be their last. After the unthinkable happened in November 1973, when Cooper of Oakengates sold out to Midland Red, the Hoggins family began to consider their own future. At the end of the year it became known that they were discussing a price for the sale of their enterprise to the NBC subsidiary, and on 7th January 1974 the deal was done. Midland Red acquired the Oakengates to Dawley service, a sprinkling of other licences for works and hospital journeys, and five vehicles (the Ford bus, two Ford coaches, and two Bedford VAM/Duple coaches). The service bus would later pass to another Telford area independent, Britannia Travel, and would spend most of its remaining life in its original working environment.

Pictured earlier with AT Brown of Trench, pre-war Dennis Lancet/Willowbrook dual-purpose vehicle CRW 327 passed to Hoggins of Wrockwardine Wood in July 1959. In September 1962 they sold it to Wolverhampton dealer Don Everall. (Roy Marshall via B Mel Gough)

Also seen earlier, both as the main subject of a Corvedale photograph and as a bystander in an Ashley of Dawley shot, 1950 Bedford OB/Mulliner bus GAW 759 came to Hoggins from the Ludlow operator in October 1954. Withdrawn in July 1963 it had a brief after-life as a mobile shop. (Roy Marshall via B Mel Gough)

A temporary replacement for GAW 759, this Crossley/Beccols coach EN 9711 (new to Auty of Bury in 1949), was acquired from Painter of Shrewsbury. It served with Hoggins for a matter of a few months, still carrying Painter fleetnames, until replaced by a new Bedford SB5/Duple Midland bus in September 1963. (Roy Marshall via B Mel Gough)

The SB5 bus, 1194 NT, gave more than ten years of service to Hoggins. The vehicle parked behind it in this 1964 view taken in Wellington is Excelsior's 3117 AC, a 1959 Bedford SB3 carrying the ugliest bodywork ever designed by Burlingham. Even Duple Midland's spartan styling looked good when parked next to it. (B Mel Gough)

# Jervis of Wellington

In the late 1920s Mr John Jervis was one of several bus proprietors based in the village of Wrockwardine Wood, to the north of Oakengates. His business began with a 14-seat Chevrolet in 1926, operating a service to Wellington, and this activity led to a share in the SOA's 'Oakengates rota'. The original Chevrolet was quickly retired in favour of a 26-seat Reo Pullman bus, delivered new in 1927, and the Reo was joined by a new 20-seat Gilford coach in 1929. A notable second-hand arrival in 1933 was a Crossley Alpha coach with 26-seat Burlingham bodywork acquired from WC Standerwick. After two years of service this machine gave way to the business's first Bedford, a new 25-seat WTL coach.

No vehicles were allocated to Jervis during the Second World War, and by the end of the conflict only the WTL survived (it would be withdrawn in 1953). From late 1945 it would be assisted by a new 32-seat Bedford OB (albeit with a 'utility style' bus body), followed by a 29-seat coach version in 1948. In 1951 the semi-utility OB was replaced by a more presentable (although third-hand) example with post-war bus bodywork which found more favour with the company's passengers.

In 1952 an AEC Regal/Duple half-cab was purchased from a neighbouring operator but was resold after a year, replaced by two 'pre-owned' OB coaches which also supplanted the pre-war WTL. The post-war OB bus was also sold soon afterwards and by the end of 1956 the Jervis fleet was made up of three Bedford OB/Duple Vista coaches which were used on the 'rota' timings, a couple of works services, and for excursions, tours, and private-hires.

In July 1958 the company doubled in size by the acquisition of the business of JH Ferrington of Wellington. 'Dumper' Ferrington (the nickname came from his ownership of a 'tipper' lorry) had entered the local coach industry in 1948 as a private-hire operator and in January 1950 had used his trading-name as the title of a new limited company, Wellington Saloon Coaches Ltd. In February 1951 he had acquired excursions and tours licences from FH Davies of Snedshill, but had swiftly surrendered that operator's 'Donnington rota' licence to concentrate on the coaching side of the purchase. In 1955 increasing legal pressure from an irate Salopia Saloon Coaches forced

Ferrington to change the name of his company to JH Ferrington & Son Ltd. At the time of the Jervis take-over his fleet consisted of two Santus-bodied Guy Arab III coaches and a Windover-bodied Foden. The Arabs were sold in late 1959, but the Foden stayed with Jervis until 1964.

One of the Ferrington Guys was replaced by a fully-fronted Burlingham-bodied AEC Regal III coach, acquired from Trent in October 1959, and twelve months later a 34-seat Regal I/Willowbrook bus was acquired from the same operator. This vehicle was usually allocated to the 'Oakengates rota' and its arrival allowed one of the two remaining OB coaches to be retired. The other was sold in mid-1962 after the arrival of an all-Leyland Royal Tiger coach from North Western, while the Regal bus was withdrawn from use in September of that year and replaced by a PS1 Tiger half-cab with 34-seat bus bodywork by Northern Coach Builders. This machine had been new to Stratford Blue but arrived in Wellington after a second career as a staff bus in the Liverpool area.

The founder died in 1960 and the business subsequently passed to a partnership of his wife Florence, his sons John Jr and Clifford and his daughter Mrs Irene Cross. In July 1964 the family decided to sell the company to Cooper of Oakengates (qv) along with its share in the 'Oakengates rota', its other licences for works services, excursions, and tours, and three vehicles; the fully-fronted Regal III coach, the Royal Tiger coach, and the PS1 Tiger service bus.

# Lowe of Hadley

Mr JE Lowe of Trench started a regular bus service from his home village to Wellington in 1927, using a 14-seat Chevrolet, and by 1931 was a member of the SOA and a participant in the 'Donnington rota' timetable. A 20-seat Bedford WLB was acquired in 1932, and was followed by another in 1934 and by a larger WTB in 1938. The only acquisitions during the Second World War were a second-hand Dennis Lancet 2 and a single OWB utility bus, while immediate post-war deliveries followed the same pattern with more pre-war Lancets and more brand-new Bedfords although the latter were OB coaches.

The new coaches were justified by the award of a licence for a seasonal express service to Llandudno. By 1948 this was being operated in a pooling arrangement with a similar route awarded to AT Brown of Trench (qv) and the two operators were jointly marketing their Llandudno operations under the 'North Wales Express Service' banner. In 1952 the business passed from the founder to his son, WHW (William) Lowe, and moved from Trench to new premises in Hadley. At one time best known for its mediaeval castle (after which its main street and various local businesses were named), the village of Hadley had latterly become famous for its engineering works where the Milnes company produced tramcars for the municipal fleets of the nation. Lowe's new base was known as the Tulip Garage and as a result the trading-name of 'Tulip Coaches' was adopted for use on all vehicles except service buses.

In 1953 the first 'Big Bedford' arrived – a brand-new SB/Duple Vega coach – but the balance was redressed in 1954 by the acquisition of another second-hand Dennis, this one a recently manufactured Falcon L6 coach with bodywork by Duple to the original Vega style. It would be the company's last Dennis and all subsequent purchases would be of Bedford manufacture, including a second-hand SB8/Duple Midland bus which replaced the Falcon on the stage-carriage route.

Ten years after assuming control of the company the second Mr Lowe decided to sell. As a condition of the North Wales pooling agreement the Llandudno licence had to be offered to AT Brown on a 'first refusal' basis and was sold to them in June 1962 along with an SB/Duple coach. The remaining two SB coaches, the SB bus, and the share in the 'Donnington rota' were sold to Smiths Eagle of Trench (qv) in July 1962.

# Martlew of Donnington Wood

William Martlew's first vehicle, a Guy delivered new in 1926, was used to inaugurate a regular service from the Donnington area to Wellington, and was followed in 1928 by two 14-seat Chevrolets. One of these was replaced in 1929 by a second (20-seat) Guy and this machine was followed by a sequence of General Motors vehicles including two more 14-seat Chevrolets, a 20-seat GMC, a Bedford WTL and a Bedford WTB.

The stage-carriage service became part of the SOA's 'Donnington rota' timetable in 1931, along with a similar route operated by H Brown of Donnington Wood (qv). The families of William Martlew and Harry Brown were related by marriage and the two operators established adjacent garages on Church Road. By then Mr Martlew had married a war widow with two teenage sons and all became active in the Martlew business.

William Martlew died at a relatively early age in 1939 and the company passed to a partnership of his (now twice widowed) wife, Mrs Annie Martlew, and her sons Richard and Albert Ashley, trading as A Martlew & Sons. Wartime deliveries were of a second-hand Dennis Lancet and two Bedford OWB utility buses, partly needed to operate new works services from the Shifnal area to industrial sites in Donnington and Hadley. These would later serve as the basis for route numbers 61-65 in the Telford New Town era.

Post-war arrivals included two Plaxton-bodied Bedford OB coaches in 1947/48 and a Beccols-bodied Crossley coach in 1949, all delivered when new. These three vehicles, along with the wartime OWBs, maintained operations until 1954 when the two utility buses were replaced by a new Bedford SBG/Duple coach and a second-hand AEC Regal/Harrington bus acquired from Newcastle Corporation. The two Plaxton-bodied OBs lasted until 1955/57 when they were replaced by an OB bus (previously used as a staff vehicle by the manufacturers) and an exceedingly odd Commer Avenger IV bus with Plaxton bodywork. The latter machine was of quite old-fashioned appearance despite being brand-new and was presumably made from components which had been stored by Plaxton for some years.

A second-hand SB/Duple coach was also acquired in 1957, while 1960 saw a sudden influx of deliveries including a 'pre-owned' Crossley coach which joined the 1949 machine, two new SB/Duple coaches, and an equally brand-new SB/Duple Midland service bus which shared the stage-carriage duties with the Avenger. A third Crossley half-cab arrived in 1963, but 1964 brought a greater surprise when the unlovable Avenger was replaced by a new 54-seat Bedford VAL/Duple Midland bus. This version of the VAL design proved as unpopular in Shropshire as elsewhere and was traded in for a 45-seat VAM coach with Duple Viscount bodywork in the summer of 1966.

Mrs Annie Martlew died in 1965 but her two

In 1958 Jervis of Wellington acquired the coaching business of JH 'Dumper' Ferrington along with three aging vehicles. Two of them were Santus-bodied Guy Arab IIIs. This is ENT 717, delivered to Ferrington in 1948. Jervis disposed of the pair in October 1959. (Roy Marshall via B Mel Gough)

The other vehicle acquired from Ferrington was this 1949 Foden PVSC6 with Windover Huntingdon coach bodywork. FUJ 93 survived in the Jervis fleet until the take-over by Cooper of Oakengates in 1964 but was not acquired by Cooper. (Roy Marshall via B Mel Gough))

The regular Jervis vehicle on the 'rota' service from October 1960 to September 1962 was this 1946 AEC Regal I with Willowbrook bus bodywork. Formerly fleet-number 731 with Trent, RC 8997 was scrapped after disposal by Jervis. (Roy Marshall via B Mel Gough)

In August 1962 Jervis acquired this 1952 all-Leyland Royal Tiger coach, FDB 605, from North Western and repainted it in this attractive variation of their standard maroon and cream livery, The Royal Tiger, along with two other Jervis vehicles, entered the Cooper fleet in July 1964. Withdrawn by them in December 1967, it went for scrap. (Roy Marshall via B Mel Gough

The Dennis Falcon L6 was intended to compete with the Bedford SB and Commer Avenger, but less than 100 were built. Duple bodied NVF 943 was new to Culling of Claxton (Norfolk) in February 1953 and passed into the Tulip Coaches fleet of Lowe of Hadley in 1954. It was replaced by a second-hand SB8/Duple Midland bus before the take-over by Smiths Eagle in 1962. (Roy Marshall via B Mel Gough)

This 1955 Bedford SBG/Duple Super Vega coach, 111 CVX, was acquired by Lowe of Hadley in 1958. It lasted for two years before being sold to dealer Don Everall. (Roy Marshall via B Mel Gough)

Martlew of Donnington Wood bought this 1946 AEC Regal I with Harrington bus bodywork from Newcastle Corporation in 1954. JVK 642 was sold on to Wessex Coaches of Bristol in 1957 and replaced by a brand-new Commer Avenger IV bus. (Roy Marshall via B Mel Gough)

EBM 606 was a Bedford OB/Duple bus, built in 1946 and retained by Vauxhall Motors for staff transportation. In December 1955 it was sold to Martlew who replaced it with a new SB1/Duple Midland bus in March 1960 and resold it to a Welsh operator. (Roy Marshall via B Mel Gough)

And here is the 1957 Avenger IV bus mentioned previously, delivered to Martlew in March 1957 as ONT 960. The Plaxton bodywork was of the same design as that fitted to Avenger I chassis in the early 1950s and was presumably a 'lowest bid' choice. In January 1964 the vehicle was sold to Carney of Rugeley and replaced by a VAL14/Duple Midland bus. (Author's Collection)

This 30 feet long Crossley/Yeates coach, MTC 347, was new to Warburton of Tottington (near Bury in Lancashire) in 1950 and arrived with Martlew from McGill of Aldridge in May 1963. Retired in January 1967, it had no further recorded user. (Author's Collection)

Bedford SB1/Duple Midland bus UUJ 394, delivered new to Martlew in March 1960, gave more than 12 years of service on the 'rota' before its retirement, a very creditable total for a lightweight chassis in everyday use on arduous local bus routes. (Roy Marshall via B Mel Gough)

And this is the VAL14/Duple Midland vehicle which replaced the Avenger IV bus in January 1964, 3170 NT. Few of this combination's recipients kept their examples for very long (largely due to problems with the VAL's braking systems in stop/go urban traffic), and Martlew's only lasted until July 1966 when it was sold to the St Helens Co-operative Society in Lancashire to perform less taxing duties. (Roy Marshall via B Mel Gough)

sons continued to use the Martlew name for the business in order to avoid any confusion with Ashley of Dawley. A second-hand VAM/Plaxton coach was acquired in 1969 and was followed by two new YRQ/Duple examples in 1972, a new YRT/Duple in 1973 and a second-hand VAL acquired from Corvedale in 1974. The company's final Bedford acquisition, a second-hand VAM with Strachan Pacemaker II service bus bodywork, was delivered in 1975, and all subsequent vehicles were coaches of Ford manufacture including one with unusual Caetano bodywork.

In May 1973 the works services between Shifnal and the Telford area were expanded to serve the new Telford Town Centre shopping complex and thrown open to the general public as services 61-65. They remained infrequent but were timed to offer convenient journeys for the businesses and schools along their paths. Less than five years later, in April 1978, the SOA 'rota' operators (with the exception of Excelsior) would agree to sell their stage-carriage routes to Midland Red. In Martlew's case only the 'Donnington rota' timings were sold, with the remainder (including services 61-65) passing to the BMB Operators consortium. In June 1978 BMB (H Brown, Martlew, and Smiths Britannia) acquired Wrekin Coach Services Ltd and used the previously dormant company as a legal entity to continue their surviving operations. WCS adopted the trading-name of Britannia Travel and so the Martlew name disappeared after more than half a century.

# Priory of Priors Lee

The village of Priors Lee, to the east of Oakengates, takes its name from the mediaeval priory which once dominated the local skyline, and when John William Jones started a bus service from the area to Wellington in 1924 the selection of Priory Motor Services as a trading name was an obvious choice. His first vehicle, a 14-seat Ford Model T, was replaced by a similarly sized Guy (acquired from Keighley Corporation) in 1927, and in 1929 a new (20-seat) Guy arrived to cope with the growing demand for the service. In 1930 the founder's two sons, John and Thomas, became involved in the business.

Membership of the SOA's 'Oakengates rota' scheme ensured a regular income and in 1936 the two Guys were replaced by two Bedfords, a second-hand WLB coach and a new WTB bus. These were supplemented during the early part of the Second World War by a third vehicle, a second-hand Dennis Mace operated from 1940-41. A Bedford OWB utility bus was delivered in 1944 and this was followed in 1948 by a brand-new OB/Duple Vista coach which replaced the two pre-war Bedfords.

The fleet remained at two vehicles for the next quarter of a century. In 1955 the wartime OWB gave way to a second-hand OB/Vista coach, and in 1960/61 the OBs were replaced by two six-year old Bedford SBGs. The first of these had conventional Duple Super Vega coach bodywork, the second was somewhat rarer as it carried a Strachan Everest body – more usually found on underfloor-engined chassis.

Control of the business passed to the two sons in 1960 and in 1964 the SBG/Duple was replaced by a newer (and diesel powered) SB1/Plaxton variant. The Strachan Everest-bodied example lasted until November 1970 when it was more than 15 years old, and the sturdiness of its bodywork had clearly made an impression upon the Jones family. The vehicle's replacement was Priory's rarest purchase of them all, a third-hand Dodge S307 with Strachan Pacemaker coach bodywork. The Dodge S300 series had been intended to challenge both the Bedford SB range and lightweight underfloor-engined types such as the Leyland Tiger Cub by offering both a front engine and a front entrance at a low purchase price. In reality its nearest competitor was the Yeates Pegasus conversion of the SB, and while the Pegasus was hardly a success in terms of sales, the Dodge was a complete flop. Production ended after less than ten vehicles had been completed, the majority for a single London coach operator which had been the original owner of the Priory machine.

The Dodge and the Plaxton-bodied SB1 maintained the 'rota' operation (and a seasonal express service to Great Yarmouth, introduced in 1964) until April 1973 when the Jones brothers decided to cease trading. The decision was undoubtedly influence by the fact that neither of their vehicles had any trade-in value to help pay for more suitable equipment. Their share in the 'Oakengates rota' passed to Excelsior of Wrockwardine Wood (qv).

Priory Motor Services of Priors Lee rarely had more than two vehicles in service at any given time. This Bedford OB/Duple Vista coach, EUX 149, was new to Priory in November 1948 and passed to a local sports club in April 1960. (Roy Marshall via B Mel Gough)

Very few Dodge S300 series PSVs were built. The first two were bus-bodied demonstrators but the only production vehicles manufactured were six S307s with Strachan Pacemaker coach bodywork for Rickards (the London coach operator), delivered in 1964. AYV 93B was one of four operated in 'British Eagle' livery for Rickards' (airline) parent company until 1968. Priory acquired it from Chambers of Uxbridge in November 1970 and used it on the 'rota' service until April 1973 when it was sold to Indigo, back in the London area. (Chris Warn Collection)

# Smiths Eagle of Trench

In the mid-1920s Mr Thomas G Smith was the proprietor of the Eagle Garage in Trench and began to offer a private-hire service which at various times used a Berliet char-a-banc and two eight-seater cars, a Lanchester and a Wolseley. By 1929 most of the journeys being operated were to Wellington and Mr Smith decided to open a regular bus service to the market town. A brand-new 20-seat Bean/Willowbrook coach was acquired for this venture, and was joined in 1931 by a second-hand 20-seat GMC bus. The original service from Trench to Wellington was incorporated into the SOA's 'Donnington rota' scheme at around the same time.

In April 1933 the Bean coach was replaced by a brand-new 32-seat Dennis Lancet and in June 1936 the GMC gave way to the first of two new Bedford WTB coaches. Wartime deliveries were mainly second-hand (including two more Dennis Lancets, two Leyland Tigers and a rare TSM double-deck chassis fitted with a single-deck coach body) although a single Bedford OWB utility bus arrived in May 1943.

The end of the war led to an influx of factory-fresh coach deliveries in 1947 including a Bedford OB/Duple Vista, two Daimler CVD6s with Associated Coach Builders bodywork and an AEC Regal III/Duple 'A' type. These replaced the pre-war WTBs, both Leyland Tigers, and one of the second-hand Lancets. The 1933 vintage Lancet and the OWB utility bus (retro-fitted with upholstered seats) continued to be the work-horses on the 'Donnington rota' service. Three more new coaches arrived in 1949 in the shape of two Crossleys with Bellhouse Hartwell bodywork and a Harrington-bodied Commer Commando.

By March 1950 the original Duple body on the 1933 Lancet was in poor condition and Smiths decided to replace it with the ACB coach body from one of the 1947 Daimler CVD6s. These bodies had been manufactured using unseasoned timber and examination showed that they would have a short service life. Both of the CVD6s were rebodied by Metalcraft, one as a half-cab and the other as a fully fronted coach. The Lancet/ACB hybrid survived until 1956 while the CVD6/Metalcraft vehicles made it into the mid-1960s.

In October 1950 Smiths Eagle acquired another 'Donnington rota' operator, Bircher & Sons of Hadley, along with a second OWB utility bus. Six months later the company entered the underfloor-engined era by purchasing a Sentinel STC4/40 bus. This vehicle proved to be profoundly unreliable and was returned to the manufacturer in September 1952. More acceptable were a pair of AEC Regal IV/Metalcraft coaches delivered in 1951/52 which gave nine years of service at Trench before being sold on for further use.

The coaching business of Leonard Ashley of Dawley (not to be confused with the stage-carriage operator Jack Ashley of the same town) was acquired in 1952. The principal attraction was a seasonal express service from the Wellington area to Blackpool, but the purchase also included excursion and tours licences and two AEC Regal III/Burlingham half-cab coaches. The arrival of these vehicles allowed the retirement and sale of the two 1949 Crossleys, which had proven to be less than ideal due to their 'problem' engines.

The company's first Bedford SB/Duple Super Vega coach arrived in May 1953, followed two months later by an almost new Dennis Falcon L6 with Yeates bodywork acquired from Auty's Tours of Bury. These additional vehicles were required due to the commencement of a new 'Forces Leave' express service from the Donnington army camp to London which drastically increased the company's coaching commitments. Deliveries for the remainder of the decade were a mixture of AEC Reliances (including a 44-seat service bus which finally replaced the 1933 Lancet) and Bedford SBs, all with bodywork by Burlingham.

In June 1958 a limited company, Smiths Eagle Coachways Ltd, was formed to replace the previous family partnership. New coaches in 1960-62 were three AEC Reliances with Duple bodywork, the first two of the 41-seat Britannia style, the last a 36-footer with a 51-seat Duple Continental body built at Burlingham's old factory in Blackpool. The other major event of 1962 was the purchase of Lowe of Hadley (qv), including an additional share in the 'Donnington rota' and three Bedford SB variants, one of them a Duple Midland-bodied bus.

The Daimler CVD6/Metalcraft half-cab was retired in the summer of 1963 and replaced by a third-hand AEC Reliance/Park Royal service bus. In the following year Smiths Eagle acquired control of AL Jones & Company of Madeley (trading as Victoria Coaches) but, unlike the company's previous acquisitions, this was kept as a separate

This Dennis Lancet 1, UJ 1441, was delivered new to Smiths Eagle of Trench in April 1933 and at that time carried a 32-seat Duple body to dual-purpose specification. In May 1950 it received a 33-seat ACB coach body from 1947 Daimler CVD6 DUX 655, which was itself re-bodied by Metalcraft. In its new clothing the Lancet lasted until January 1956. Note the distinctive Metalcraft beading beneath the windows, added at the time of the body-swap. (Roy Marshall via B Mel Gough)

Commer Commando/Harrington coach EUX 959 served with Smiths Eagle from new in February 1949 until the early 1970s. It was later preserved by well-known enthusiast and bus operator Martin Perry who painted it into his own livery for further PSV use. (Author's Collection)

Metalcraft's work on the pre-war Dennis Lancet and the two post-war Daimler CVD6s led to an order for two more coach bodies in 1951/52, both on new AEC Regal IV chassis. The 1952 machine, HUX 350, stayed with Smiths Eagle until May 1961. After sale it gave further service to Jewitt of Spennymoor in County Durham. (Roy Marshall via B Mel Gough)

Seen here on a 'Donnington rota' timing, Bedford SBG/Burlingham coach NNT 588 was one of two delivered to Smiths Eagle in March 1956. It gave 15 years of service before going to Squire of Willenhall in 1971. (Author's Collection)

The replacement for the pre-war Lancet arrived in July 1956 in the shape of a brand-new AEC Reliance/Burlingham service bus, NUX 256. It was still in the fleet when the end came in April 1978 and was scrapped in the Ludlow area later in the same year. (Geoff Mills)

Reliance/Park Royal bus PCY 546 was new to Thomas Bros of Port Talbot in December 1957 and saw service with Gloucestershire independent Silvey of Epney before passing to Smiths Eagle in June 1963. Although withdrawn from use in 1973 it was kept at the garage as a source of spares for NUX 256 and was later scrapped alongside it at Ludlow. (Author's Collection)

subsidiary. Another significant development, in 1966, was the formation of Wrekin Coach Services Ltd (basically a booking agency) in collaboration with Cooper of Oakengates, Elcock of Ironbridge and Hoggins of Wrockwardine Wood. The Blackpool service was included in this pooling arrangement and Smiths Eagle acquired a new Ford R192/Duple Viscount coach to demonstrate their commitment to the new consortium. This vehicle was followed by a second-hand SB5/Duple Bella Vega, a new VAM5/Duple Viceroy (in 1968) and a one-year old Leyland Leopard with a 53-seat Plaxton body which replaced the earlier Reliance/Duple Continental 36-footer in August 1970.

In March 1970 Victoria Coaches of Madeley changed its name to Telford Coachways Ltd and adopted the parent company's livery of dark green and beige to emphasise the connection to Smiths Eagle. Unusual vehicle acquisitions during the early 1970s included a pair of Leyland/Weymann LW2 Olympian 44-seat service buses. These came from Western Welsh (the major customer for the type) in March 1971, and one of them received Telford Coachways titles for the subsidiary's stage-carriage operations in Madeley.

Trouble was on the horizon. In November 1973 Cooper of Oakengates sold out to Midland Red and at a Wrekin Coach Services board meeting Hoggins of Wrockwardine Wood announced that they would shortly follow suit. The remaining two shareholders in WCS, Smiths Eagle and Elcock of Ironbridge, were forced to consider their alternatives. They decided to remain in alliance and as a token of their continuing co-operation it was agreed that Telford Coachways would be sold to Elcock, with whom it had previously competed. Operations on the 'Donnington rota' seemed quite stable by comparison and another service bus, a second-hand Bedford VAM70 with Willowbrook bodywork, arrived in 1975 to replace the surviving LW2 Olympian.

The writing was nevertheless on the wall after the defection of Cooper and Hoggins, and on 1st April 1978 the surviving members of the SOA sold their famous 'rota' services to Midland Red. While some of the Telford area operators continued in business (eg AT Brown and Excelsior) and others huddled together for warmth in the new operational environment (H Brown, Martlew, and Smiths Britannia), the descendants of Thomas

G Smith decided to call it a day. The valuable Blackpool licence was also sold to Midland Red, Smiths Eagle's other coaching activities were merged into those of Elcock/Telford Coachways, and Wrekin Coach Services (which no longer served any purpose) was sold as a 'shell company' to the Brown/Martlew/Britannia grouping to serve as the legal basis of their own new enterprise. Smiths Eagle ceased to exist but is still fondly remembered and has a 'living' memorial in the shape of the immaculately preserved Daimler CVD6/Metalcraft coach DUX 655.

# William Smith & Successors

AW (William) Smith bought a 14-seat Ford Model T in May 1924 and used it to start a regular bus service from Donnington Wood to Wellington via Oakengates. By 1931 the route had been incorporated into the SOA's 'Oakengates rota'. Pre-war vehicles were mainly of Chevrolet/GMC/Bedford manufacture but in 1934 a 32-seat Dennis Lancet was acquired and would become the mainstay of the stage-carriage route for more than two decades.

The strategic importance of the Donnington area led to the allocation of two Bedford OWB utility buses during the Second World War, although the first had been sold before the second one arrived. After the end of the war second-hand purchases included another 32-seat Dennis Lancet bus and a 26-seat Dennis Arrow, both in 1946. A more important development came in September 1947 when Smith acquired the business of GA Darrall of Dawley (trading as Supreme Motor Services) along with 'non-rota' stage-carriage services from Dawley to Oakengates (via two routes) and from Dawley to Wellington. Only one vehicle, a wartime OWB, was included in the deal but the licences were virtually priceless and more than doubled Smith's stage-carriage mileage overnight. Several second-hand Bedfords were acquired to cover the additional work.

In 1948 a brand-new service from Oakengates to Dawley was approved by the Traffic Commissioners, taking a more westerly route via Ketley in preference to the Ketley Bank option taken by the two former Darrall services. A year later the founder, until then a sole proprietor, took his four sons (William Jr, Frederick, George and Edward) into partnership to help run the growing family enterprise.

Very old Dennis Lancets were a common sight on the SOA 'rotas' in the mid-1950s. Besides CRW 327 (operated by AT Brown and then Hoggins) and UJ 1441 (of Smiths Eagle) there was this fine example, UJ 2642. Delivered new to William Smith in 1934 with a 32-seat bus body, it received a new 32-seat coach body by WS Yeates after the war and continued in service until 1958. (B Mel Gough Collection)

The re-bodied Lancet's replacement was a re-bodied AEC Regal I. The 1946 chassis of DUK 752 received a new Burlingham body in 1953 and is seen in service with W Smith & Sons shortly before the company was taken over by Hoggins of Wrockwardine Wood in March 1959. Hoggins sold the vehicle to Leadbetter of Sutton Coldfield three months later. (Roy Marshall via B Mel Gough)

More expansion came in July 1951 when the Smiths acquired the business of HR (Reg) Evason including another share in the 'Oakengates rota', a pre-war Bedford WTB bus and a post-war OB fitted with a wartime utility body. Another significant purchase during 1951 was a pair of pre-war Leyland TS8 Tiger buses with ECW bodywork, acquired from Yorkshire Traction. They gave good service on the stage routes until their withdrawal in 1954/55, operating alongside the 1934 Lancet which had been rebodied by Yeates in 1947.

In 1953 the founder died without leaving a clear indication of his plans for the succession. His widow, Lily May Smith, formed a partnership with his sons, William and Frederick, to continue the business, but the other two sons were determined to strike out on their own and demanded that the assets should be divided to cater for this possibility. In the wake of this dispute the Dawley to Wellington route was sold to Jack Ashley (qv), possibly to pay off the death duties on the founder's estate, while the Oakengates to Dawley via Ketley route passed to George Smith and the share in the 'Oakengates rota' to his brother Edward. The vehicles were also split up, with George receiving a WTB and an OWB and Edward a post-war OB/Mulliner bus. Mrs Smith, William Jr and Frederick (still trading as W Smith & Sons) retained the two Oakengates to Dawley via Ketley Bank routes, three Bedfords, the surviving TS8 Tiger and the 1934 Lancet which survived until 1958 with its new Yeates body.

The Lancet's eventual replacement was a 1946 AEC Regal I which had been fitted with a Burlingham 'Seagull style' body in 1953 and this was soon joined by another fully-fronted coach, a Crossley with Windover bodywork. They were destined to be the last purchases by the original company. In March 1959 the Oakengates-Ketley Bank-Dawley services and the business's three remaining vehicles were sold to Hoggins of Wrockwardine Wood (qv). This left the two 'autonomous' brothers, George and Edward, as the surviving representatives of their family's briefly burgeoning empire.

George Smith quickly replaced his 'inherited' vehicles with newer models, an OB/Mulliner bus acquired from LG Phillips of Glynceiriog in 1957 and a famously ugly OB with Willenhall bodywork which was shooed away by Ashley of Dawley in

1958. The Willenhall vehicle was replaced by a more orthodox OB/Duple Vista coach in 1961, and was deemed unfit for any further use bar scrap metal.

Meanwhile, Edward Smith had also splashed out on replacement equipment in 1957 and had made two slightly unusual purchases of his own in the shape of a fully-fronted OB/Plaxton coach and one of the very few Bedford SBs to receive bodywork by Metalcraft. To make the latter vehicle even more peculiar its new owner removed its original (seized) Bedford petrol engine and replaced it with an Albion diesel unit acquired from the dealer Don Everall. The OB/Plaxton was sold in 1961 but the Bedford/Metalcraft/Albion combination survived until April 1962 when it was sold (along with the 'Oakengates rota' service) to Cooper of Oakengates (qv). Edward Smith then took a long break before returning to the local PSV industry as a private-hire operator in September 1963, using a single OB/Duple Vista coach. This enterprise continued until October 1968, but from late 1964 was one of two businesses receiving Edward Smith's attentions.

George Smith's health had been failing for some time and in November 1964 he proposed a new partnership with his brother Edward to operate the Oakengates-Ketley-Dawley service. This materialised as Smith Brothers and later included their respective sons, George Edward Sidney Smith and Gerald Edward Smith. George Sr decided to retire in March 1968, taking his son with him, and the business passed to Edward Smith and his son Gerald. Edward was also ready for retirement and as a result Gerald Smith became the sole proprietor in October of the same year. To complicate matters further, Gerald had already been in business in his own right as a private-hire operator since May 1966, operating a single Bedford SB/Duple coach.

The final 'Smith Brothers' vehicle on the Dawley service had been an SBG/Duple coach acquired from Excelsior in 1967 to replace the last OB. Under Gerald's proprietorship this was replaced by a 40-seat SB/Duple Midland bus acquired from a Gloucestershire operator. In April 1971 this gave way to a Willowbrook-bodied Albion Aberdonian bus which came from Venture of Consett. The following year brought a new fleetname when Gerald Smith decided to trade as Smith's Britannia Coaches to avoid any possible

This fully-fronted Plaxton-bodied Bedford OB, EUJ 118, was new to Martlew in June 1948 and passed to Edward Smith in December 1957. Four years later Mr Smith sold it to Cantello of Birmingham for further service. (B Mel Gough Collection)

Very few Bedford SBs were bodied by Metalcraft but this 35-seat coach, BFA 687, was delivered to a Staffordshire operator in 1953. A dealer replaced its original Bedford petrol engine with an Albion diesel unit in 1957 and sold it to Edward Smith. Taken over by Cooper in April 1962 along with Smith's 'rota' service, it lasted for another three years despite its mongrel genes. (Roy Marshall via B Mel Gough)

George Smith acquired this 1949 Bedford OB/Mulliner bus, FUN 415, from LG Phillips of Glynceiriog in June 1957 but scrapped it only two years later. It was 'Fun' while it lasted! (B Mel Gough Collection)

Willenhall Coachcraft produced the bodywork for around a dozen 'small Bedfords' between 1948 and 1950, all but one to an amusingly eccentric Art Deco design. The oven-ready turkey amid the origami swans was SRE 908, an OB delivered to Bassett of Tittensor in 1949. It passed to Ashley of Dawley in 1952 and then to George Smith (as seen here) in June 1958. He used it for another three years before ending its wretched existence. (Roy Marshall via B Mel Gough)

Gerald Smith bought this 1958 Albion Aberdonian/Willowbrook service bus, 165 BUP, from its original owner, Venture of Consett, in April 1971. Three years later he sold it to Davies of Tredegar. (RF Mack via B Mel Gough)

From 1972 onwards Gerald Smith traded as 'Smiths Britannia Coaches'. This Ford R192/Willowbrook bus, XKG 762K, arrived from France of Cardiff in 1975 and in June 1978 was one of nine Smiths Britannia vehicles transferred to the new Wrekin Coach Services Ltd fleet (trading as Britannia Travel) for residual works and schools contracts. (Roy Marshall via B Mel Gough)

confusion with neighbouring operator Smiths Eagle. In 1973 the Aberdonian, never the most satisfactory of machines and rapidly approaching its 'sell by date', was replaced by a brand-new Ford/Willowbrook service bus. Two more or less identical vehicles would arrive over the next five years along with half a dozen Ford coaches.

When the SOA members decided to sell their stage-carriage routes to Midland Red in 1978 Gerald Smith took the opportunity to follow their lead. The Oakengates-Ketley-Dawley route, the final remnant of the family's stage-carriage network, passed to Midland Red on 1st April 1978. In conjunction with the proprietors of H Brown and Martlew, the other two Donnington Wood survivors, Gerald Smith formed the BMB Operators grouping to continue beyond the Midland Red take-over. In June 1978 the partners acquired a more or less dormant company, Wrekin Coach Services Ltd, from the owners of Smiths Eagle and Elcock and used it as the legal foundation for their new operation. As Smith's Britannia Coaches had contributed more vehicles to the new company than H Brown and Martlew combined, WCS took the trading-name of Britannia Travel and used the mainly blue livery previously favoured by Gerald Smith's company.

At first the newly combined operation concentrated on excursions, extended tours (as 'Britannia International Travel'), schools and works services and private-hires, but after deregulation would also become involved in the bidding for 'tendered' local bus services. The company expanded rapidly as a result and had more than doubled the size of its fleet by the end of 2001. It was a good time to sell the business and in 2002 ownership passed from the Ashley, Brown and Smith families to Lionspeed Ltd, owned by the same group of investors as deregulation newcomer Pete's Travel. Sadly, the new management of Britannia proved to be less capable than their predecessors, contracts were lost as a result of unreliable operation, and in 2004 the company went into liquidation. It was a regrettable end for such a fascinating company and severed the last historical links to Brown's proud Sentinel fleet, Martlew's archaic Avenger/Plaxton bus and George Smith's truly horrible Willenhall bodied OB. At least in this book we can still enjoy them all as if they were trapped in amber.

# Victoria of Madeley

In 1926 Mrs Alice L Jones of Madeley took delivery of a brand-new 14-seat Chevrolet char-a-banc, employing it on private-hire work and on a (Thursday only) market-day service to Wellington. Two Chevrolet buses followed and in September 1930 the original char-a-banc was replaced by a 20-seat GMC. Many of the journeys operated by Jones carried workers to local industrial sites, and the economic depression which followed the Wall Street Crash in 1929 had a profoundly deleterious effect upon demand for her services. To save the business she took several members of her family into partnership, including her two sons and her daughter (Mrs EO Bullock) but by the end of 1931 the fleet had shrunk from three to two vehicles, the GMC and a 26-seat Guy.

A second 'shoppers' service, a Wednesday-only run from Ironbridge to Wolverhampton via Madeley and Shifnal, had started in 1930 and this helped to keep the business alive, but the bulk of its revenues continued to come from workers bound for destinations such as Granville and Kemberton Collieries, the Buildwas power station and the Sankey works at Hadley.

By 1937 the local economy had recovered to the point where a brand-new Bedford WTB could be bought, and for more than twenty years all purchases were of Bedford manufacture. At around this time the company began to use the trading name of Victoria Coaches, reflecting the location of its garage in Victoria Road, Madeley.

The Second World War brought a sudden surge of vehicles including two second-hand WTBs and three OWB utility buses. Both of the 'shoppers' services were suspended for the duration of hostilities, and while the Wolverhampton service resumed in 1946 (it would end in 1952), the dormant Wellington route was replaced in 1947 by a Saturday-only run to Dawley. Mrs Alice Jones died in 1947 and the business passed into the stewardship of her daughter-in-law, Mrs Doris Jones. In 1948 the surviving members of the Jones and Bullock families established a limited company, AL Jones & Co Ltd (still trading as Victoria Coaches) and in 1950 the firm received approval for a new stage-carriage service from Coalport to Hodge Bower via Madeley. This operated on every day except Sunday and passed many important industrial sites in the area.

The post-war fleet was made up entirely of

Bedford OBs and SBs until 1960 when a ten-year old Commer Avenger coach with Plaxton bodywork arrived. Other changes were afoot. In 1964 the founding family sold the business to Smiths Eagle Coachways of Trench (qv) which continued to operate it as a subsidiary company with its own identity. Six years later it became Telford Coachways Ltd and the Victoria name was dropped, as was the traditional red and cream livery which gave way to Smiths Eagle's preferred combination of dark green and beige. The early 1970s also witnessed the arrival of the first service buses in the fleet since the departure of the last OWB in 1956. One was an ex-Western Welsh LW2 Olympian, the other a Marshall-bodied Tiger Cub from Yorkshire Woollen District.

In November 1973 the company changed hands again when Smiths Eagle sold it to MH Elcock & Son of Ironbridge, a coach operator which had competed with the Jones/Victoria/Telford Coachways enterprise since 1928. Elcock repainted the vehicles in their own livery (red) but with additional 'Telford Coachways' fleet-names. The end finally came in September 1980 when Elcock moved their own headquarters from Ironbridge to Madeley and merged the subsidiary's vehicles into the main fleet.

# Williams of Wrockwardine Wood

In the 1920s the small village of Wrockwardine Wood, to the north of Oakengates, could probably claim to be the home of more stage-carriage operators than any other similarly sized community in Britain. Among the umpteen proprietors was James W Williams, who started operations between Lamb Corner and Wellington via Oakengates in 1924 with a 14-seat Ford Model T acquired three years earlier for private-hire use. The Ford was replaced by a Chevrolet in 1925 and this was traded in for a 20-seat GMC in 1928. Membership of the SOA and a share in the 'Oakengates rota' gave the business a measure of stability, and in 1934 a new Bedford WLB replaced the GMC. This was replaced in turn by a larger 26-seat WTB bus in 1938.

At the beginning of the Second World War Mr Williams was still a one-horse operator, but the large military and industrial facilities in the area soon required an increase in the fleet size. A second-hand WTB coach arrived in late 1939, followed by a Plaxton-bodied Leyland Cub in 1940. A fourth vehicle arrived in early 1942 in the shape of a Park Royal-bodied Leyland Tiger coach acquired from East Kent, while at the end of the same year the WTB coach was replaced by a more suitable OWB utility bus.

In 1947 two new Bedford OB buses arrived to replace the Cub and the OWB, along with an OB/Duple Vista coach to refresh the private-hire and excursion part of the business. Another OB/Vista was delivered in 1948 in exchange for one of the 1947 bus versions, and in 1949 the pre-war WTB bus was retired to make room in the garage for a third OB/Vista and a 33-seat Crossley/Burlingham coach, both acquired when new. The bus/coach balance was restored in June 1951 by the acquisition of an 'upgraded' OWB from a Yorkshire operator. In August 1951 the founder's son, Cyril, became a partner and the business started to trade as JW Williams & Son. Its first Bedford SB (a Yeates Riviera-bodied coach which replaced the Crossley) arrived in July 1953, and Bedford vehicles held a monopoly in the fleet after 1955 when the East Kent Tiger was finally retired.

Cyril Williams became the sole proprietor in 1965 and by 1970 was operating three Bedford SB coaches, all of them acquired on the second-hand market. One of these, the newest of the trio, was traded in for a second-hand Bedford VAM/Plaxton coach in 1971. The other two SBs were replaced by brand-new Bedford YRQ coaches in 1972/75, one with Plaxton bodywork and the other with a more unusual body by Caetano. None of these vehicles was particularly suitable for stage-carriage work (and impossible to modify for 'driver only' operation), so Mr Williams began to consider his options. From 1977 the 'Oakengates rota' timings were operated by vehicles on hire from Martlew of Donnington Wood (qv) and this arrangement continued until the end of the SOA's 'rota' operations on 1st April 1978.

With the 'rota' service gone and Midland Red vehicles everywhere it became obvious that the Williams business was too small to survive in the new environment, and in June 1978 the remainder was sold to Wrekin Coach Services Ltd, trading as Britannia Travel.

Photographs of vehicles belonging to Victoria Coaches (AL Jones) of Madeley were difficult to find, so this shot of their rarest machine was particularly welcome. Churchill-bodied Bedford SB HAW 838 was one of a pair built for an unidentified dealer in 1951. Identical twin HAW 837 went to Vagg of Knockin Heath, while '838 served briefly with Charles of Cleobury Mortimer and Bradley of Kidderminster before arriving in Madeley in September 1952. It stayed with Victoria for five years before resale to a Devonshire operator. (Chris Elmes Collection)

Williams of Wrockwardine Wood frequently made use of coaches on their 'rota' timings, including Bedford OB/ Duple Vista FNT 861, new to Williams in September 1949. In this garage shot the vehicle is parked next to SBG/ Super Vega HBW 306, another 'rota' regular, and both are in the operator's attractive red and pale blue livery. (Author's Collection)

# Part Four
# *THE CHICKEN PLUCKERS' BUSES*

In the heavily regulated era covered by this book there were three kinds of "works services". The first category consisted of routes which (while primarily aimed at the employees of a specific company) were also available for use by the general public and collected fares from all on board. These required licences in the normal way. The second type of services also charged fares (often subsidised by the employer) but were restricted to employees of the company involved. Once again, licences were required. A third category was restricted to employees, made no charge to passengers, and was operated by vehicles belonging to the employer, and these latter services could operate entirely legally without a licence.

The ground rules for inclusion in this book (along with its predecessor covering Staffordshire) would normally eliminate all operators of services in the second and third categories by defining an "Independent Bus" as one available to the general public. However, rules are made to be broken in exceptional circumstances and it is hard to think of a more exceptional case than that of the JP Wood company, based at The Grove in Craven Arms, deep in the rural depths of southern Shropshire.

JP Wood & Sons (Poultry) Ltd, trading as "Chukie Chicken", was a long-established but modestly sized business until 1956 when the proprietors decided to expand beyond their local horizons and become a nationwide supplier. The obvious problem was that of attracting a vastly enlarged work-force in an area with minimal levels of public transport, especially when most of the potential employees would have no access to a car and no prospect of buying one given the meagre wages on offer. Wood's decided to operate their own fleet of buses as a solution.

In the late 1950s and the 1960s most of the vehicles operated were time-expired coaches, ranging from elderly half-cabs to slightly more modern Bedford SBs. The "route network" included three services to Shrewsbury (via an assortment of villages) and others to Bishops Castle, Church Stretton, Clun, Ironbridge, Knighton, Ludlow and Much Wenlock, requiring a fleet of around a dozen vehicles.

In 1968 the company was acquired by Unilever and by the early 1970s the work-force had grown to more than a thousand. The original half-cabs disappeared, replaced by a mixture of London Transport exiles (five RFs and three GSs) and second-hand AEC Reliances (which came from City of Oxford, Maidstone & District and North Western). All of these vehicles offered full destination blinds and the JP Wood services began to display route numbers (the Shrewsbury services, for example, were the 41/42/46).

From 1974 onwards a substantial fleet of minibuses was acquired to operate alongside the former PSVs. Later in the same decade the RFs, GSs and Reliances would be replaced in their turn by a profusion of Bristol/ECW types including LS buses from Western National, MW buses from Red & White and Southern Vectis, FLF Lodekkas from Crosville and Hants & Dorset and RELL buses from Crosville and Red & White. The Bristol/ECW theme continued into the early 1980s with the arrival of LH buses from Hants & Dorset. In April 1981 the company applied for route licences for the first time, intending to start charging its employees for their transportation. Trade union objections ensured that this never happened and the services continued as a private (and free) operation until the very end.

The late 1980s saw the FLFs supplanted by two early model VRTs from South Midland and two Alexander-bodied Fleetlines from Strathtay, but frozen chickens from elsewhere in Europe were already invading the British market and as sales of "Chukie Chicken" fell so did the workforce. In 1991 the "full-size" bus fleet was withdrawn. The minibuses continued for a while but by the end of 1993 the company had ceased to exist as if it had all been a glorious dream.

JP Wood's early fleet contained an eclectic mixture of aging coaches including this pre-war AEC Regal with a post-war Harrington body and the 1950 registration KTG 23. In use with Wood's from 1958 until 1968, it is seen at the depot in The Grove, Craven Arms. (Chris Warn Collection)

Parked next to the Regal shown above, FAW 991 was a Foden PVFE6 with Metalcraft bodywork, originally delivered to Salopia of Whitchurch in 1949 as their fleet number 62. Acquired by JP Wood in 1959, it retained its Salopia colour scheme of distemper green and primer grey. (Chris Warn Collection)

JP Wood's first livery, as shown on Regal KTG 23 and on this 1950 PS2 Tiger with Burlingham Sunsaloon bodywork, NDH 738, was a rather tasteful combination of grey with black relief. The Tiger came to The Grove from Spencer of Birmingham in 1960 and lasted until 1968. The titles on the side read "Chukie Brand Poultry". (Chris Warn Collection)

In the later (1973) light blue and cream livery, along with "Chukie chicken and turkey" titles, this is Park Royal-bodied Reliance 756 KFC which had a highly appropriate registration for a chicken bus! The vehicle migrated to The Grove in 1973 from City of Oxford and became JP Wood's fleet number 13. It was withdrawn from use by them in 1981 and is now preserved in City of Oxford's pre-NBC livery. (Chris Warn Collection)

# Part Five
# *SHROPSHIRE IN COLOUR*

As a bus enthusiast based in Manchester in the 1960s I thanked my lucky stars for the variety provided by the smaller municipal operators. Without them everything in sight would have been red in one shade or another, particularly in the hallowed precincts of Lower Mosley Street bus station where the only relief was provided by the blue of Ashton-under-Lyne and the green of SHMD on service 6 to Glossop. Red is a perfectly acceptable colour, but one can see too much of it in the course of a single day.

In Shropshire the alternative colours were provided by the independents which offered an entire spectrum of contrasting hues to alleviate the boredom of Crosville's drab 'Tilling Green' and Midland Red's all too literal interpretation of its fleetname. Oswestry on a busy market-day, for example, offered many vehicles in Crosville's unimaginative corporate colour scheme but an equal number in assorted varieties of brown (Gittins), maroon (Hampson), blue (Hyde, Fisher, and Bryn Melyn), light green (Bartley), orange and black (Parish), and red with a dark green top (Vagg).

In Shrewsbury the monobloc red of the area-agreement company would have been unbearable without the varying blues of Minsterley and Mid-Wales, the distinguished dark green of Williamson, the tasteful brown and cream of Boulton, the distinctive (red, brown and cream) colours of Valley and the unpredictable offerings of Worthen Motorways. Even Salopia's uninspiring livery of green and grey looked better when providing a welcome counterpoint to the relentless red of BMMO.

Wellington was (theoretically) another Midland Red town, but at most times the BET subsidiary's vehicles were out-numbered by far more attractively painted machines. The green fleets included AT Brown, H Brown and Smiths Eagle; the red fleets (all of them more imaginatively attired than BMMO could manage) included Ashley, Excelsior, Martlew and Priory. Cooper favoured orange and brown, Hoggins black and white and Williams a surprisingly pleasing mixture of red and light blue. By comparison the Midland Red fleet looked as if it had been painted in an automatic bus-wash. The black tops of the company's coaches and dual-purpose vehicles helped a little, but not a lot.

In this all too limited selection of colour views the images are presented in the same order as the operators' histories in the main text, with vehicles from 'Oswestry & The North' (in alphabetical order) followed by those from 'Shrewsbury & The South', and then by those from the 'Wellington & Telford' area. Many of the original photographers remain unknown, but all are thanked for their roles in recording an essential (and often overlooked) aspect of the bus industry's rich and fascinating history. I hope that you enjoy their work as much as I did.

This 1954 Leyland Tiger Cub/Burlingham Seagull, HFR 603, came to Butter of Childs Ercall from its original owner, WC Standerwick of Blackpool, in May 1967 and was withdrawn from service in March 1971. (Geoff Lumb via Eric Wain)

The Gittins brothers' pride and joy, 1954 Royal Tiger/Seagull coach KNT 780, is seen at Llandudno in the summer of 1966, At the end of that year the Gittins would retire and the vehicle would pass to Vagg of Knockin Heath. It appears again on the back cover in Boulton livery. (Vic Nutton)

Hampson's famous 'private-hire RFs' were finally replaced by a pair of Bristol LH6L/ECW buses acquired from Trent. Never repainted into Vagg livery, they passed to Robert Lunt's 'Hampson 82' operation after the collapse of Vagg's parent company. (Author's Collection)

Hyde's Ellesmere depot circa 1965 with OB/Duple Vista coach FNT 88 on the right, OB/Duple bus GUJ 291 on the left, and Commer minibus 644 NT in the background. The garage would later be used by Fisher of Bronington and then by Lakeside. (Geoff Lumb via Chris Elmes)

Parish's yard at Morda in the early 1970s, featuring ex-LUT Reliance/Plaxton Highway dual-purpose vehicle 272 STF, Bedford SB5/Duple Bella Vega BND 153C and an unidentified livestock transporter. (Malcolm Yeomans Collection)

Salopia of Whitchurch's Bedford SB5/Duple Midland bus YAW 166 is seen in Shrewsbury awaiting departure to its home town. The company's notoriously uninspiring livery is not helped by the replacement side panel in the wrong colour! (Chris Elmes Collection)

Vagg of Knockin Heath was the only Shropshire independent to receive brand-new double-deckers, in the shape of two all-Leyland PD2/1 highbridge models delivered in 1950. GAW 700 awaits departure from Oswestry with Hampson's 'private-hire RF' LUC 212 on their 'Town' service visible behind it. (Vic Nutton)

A pair of Vagg's ex-Crosville Bedford OB/Duple Vista coaches seen resting at Knockin Heath. These 1949 vehicles were sold to Vagg in March 1960. KFM 429 (in the foreground) lasted until February 1969, KFM 432 (to its left) until June 1967. (Vic Nutton)

In November 1967 Vagg's all-Leyland PD2s were replaced by a pair of 1954 AEC Regent III/Park Royal double-deckers with platform doors, acquired from City of Oxford. UWL 940 was withdrawn from use and scrapped in 1972. (B Mel Gough Collection)

After receiving six Bristol SC4LK/ECW buses from Eastern National in 1964, Vagg acquired a pair of the much rarer dual-purpose versions from Victoria of Leigh-on-Sea in February 1969. They had been new to Eastern Counties in 1956. TVF 869 was withdrawn and scrapped during 1973. (B Mel Gough Collection)

AEC Reliance/Park Royal dual-purpose vehicle WLW 42 was new to Birch Bros of London NW5 in 1959 as their fleet number K42. Acquired by Vagg in March 1970, it was withdrawn from service in 1974. (B Mel Gough Collection)

This 1968 Bedford VAM/Duple Midland bus, SMC 519F, came to Vagg from Royal of Redditch in 1974. After three years at Knockin Heath it was sold to McSorley of Eardington. (B Mel Gough Collection)

Corvedale of Ludlow acquired this 1957 Bedford SB8/Duple Midland bus, RWO 840, from Jones of Aberbeeg in January 1962 and kept it until September 1963 when it was sold to Griffiths (Teme Valley) of Leintwardine. The BMMO S15 behind it is on the Ludlow-Bridgnorth service which Midland Red acquired from Corvedale in 1953. (Author's Collection)

When Albert Davies (Transport) of Acton Burnell withdrew from the bus and coach business in July 1965 this 1949 Crossley/Plaxton coach, FAW 334, was placed into long-term storage by the Davies family. Two decades later it was restored to its original condition and became a regular visitor to vehicle rallies. (Chris Elmes)

Minsterley Motors ran a mixture of new and second-hand coaches on their stage-carriage services in the 1960s and 1970s, including 1962 Bedford SB8/Duple Super Vega 704 RDH. The vehicle arrived from Morris of Borehamwood in March 1967, still wearing the livery of original owner Central Coachways, and remained with Minsterley until the mid-1980s. (Chris Elmes)

This 1963 Bedford SB5/Duple Midland bus, 1877 NT, was new to Shropshire County Council as a dedicated schools service vehicle. In 1976 it was sold to Minsterley Motors and is seen here at their Stiperstones depot shortly after its arrival. It was later repainted into standard blue and cream colours. (Chris Elmes)

Delivered to Lothian in 1975 this Bedford YRT/Alexander Y-type bus, GSX 117N, passed to Minsterley in 1982. It is seen here on Welsh Bridge in Shrewsbury on its way back to its rural base. (Chris Elmes)

Despite appearances this 1966 Bedford VAM/Duple Bella Venture coach, JBW 527D, was never in the Minsterley fleet. After retirement by Boulton of Cardington the vehicle was acquired by preservationist Chris Elmes who restored it to 'Class VI' status (in 'Swain's Coaches' livery) for heritage private-hire work. Chris is married to the grand-daughter of WJT Swain, the pioneer of stage services in the area and predecessor of Minsterley Motors. (Chris Elmes)

Ford R192/Willowbrook bus TAW 432J was new to Valley Motors in October 1970 and is pictured in Barker Street, Shrewsbury, in the early 1970s on the main service to Bishops Castle. To the right is Worthen Motorways' Ford VUX 576K on the Montgomery route, which would soon pass to Valley. In 1982 Valley's Bishops Castle operations, including TAW 432J, were sold to Minsterley. (Chris Elmes)

Valley acquired Worthen Motorways in 1974 and from 1982 the remainder of the company's operations were based at Worthen. As the previously operated Ford service buses had passed to Minsterley replacements were required and this 1974 Bedford YRT/Willowbrook bus, RBD 108M, was one of two acquired from United Counties. It retained their leaf green and white NBC livery without any visible titles. (Chris Elmes)

At first sight EP 9031 would seem to be a Bedford OB, but it is in fact a 1946 OLBD lorry chassis fitted with Mulliner bus bodywork in 1949 for Williamson of Shrewsbury. Seen in Barker Street, it lasted until February 1967 and was then sold for further (non-PSV) use. (Vic Nutton)

New to Stringfellow of Wigan in 1957, Bedford SB8/Yeates Europa coach DJP 20 passed to Excelsior of Wrockwardine Wood in April 1962 and then to Worthen Motorways in January 1965. In this early 1970s shot it still retains its Excelsior colour scheme, Worthen having abandoned the concept of a fleet livery shortly before its arrival. (Chris Elmes)

This Sentinel STC4/40, GUJ 608, started life as a company demonstrator in 1950. It later passed to Maryland Coaches in London, then to Warner of Tewkesbury, and from them to H Brown of Donnington Wood in February 1959. Withdrawn by Brown in the early 1970s it passed into preservation, and is currently on display at the Aston Manor transport museum in Birmingham in its original blue and cream demonstrator livery. (B Mel Gough)

Brown's long love affair with Sentinels had started in 1951 with the delivery of five SLC4/35 coach variants with Beadle bodywork. Originally equipped with centre entrances, all but one were converted to front entrance for 'driver only' operation during the mid-1960s. This is HAW 302 on the 'Donnington rota' service in front of Brown's 1971 Bedford YRQ/Willowbrook bus UNT 915J. (B Mel Gough)

The last of Cooper of Oakengates' large fleet of Crossley SD42s were withdrawn in late 1964/early 1965. This one, 1950 Metalcraft-bodied example GAW 382, survived until October 1964 and was later scrapped (with most of its shed-fellows) at Ketley Steel Works. (B Mel Gough Collection)

A colour shot of a black and white vehicle! Hoggins' famous Morris Commercial OPR/Plaxton coach JMU 297 (with Pilot Coaches titles) is seen on the Dawley route in the early 1960s. Acquired from Pride of the West, Weston-super-Mare, in April 1961 it gave three years of service before passing to the scrapman. (B Mel Gough Collection)

This 1948 PS1 Tiger/NCB bus, GUE 253, was originally delivered to Stratford Blue and in 1960 passed to a Liverpool company for use as a staff vehicle. In October 1962 it returned to PSV service with Jervis of Wellington (as seen here) and was one of three vehicles taken over by Cooper of Oakengates in July 1964. Cooper kept it for a year before scrapping it. (B Mel Gough Collection)

Lowe of Hadley bought this 1957 Bedford SB8/Duple Midland bus, VTG 739, from Thomas of Barry in 1961. After just over a year in Lowe's red and cream livery it passed with the business to Smiths Eagle of Trench in July 1962. (B Mel Gough Collection)

Bedford SBG 457 EMC, new to Anglo-Continental Motorways in 1955, was unusual in carrying Strachan Everest bodywork. Priory Motor Services of Priors Lee acquired it from Evans of Senghennyd in March 1961 and used it on their 'rota' service until November 1970. Visible behind it is a Gliderways AEC Reliance/Harrington Cavalier coach. (B Mel Gough Collection)

Daimler CVD6 coach DUX 655 was one of a pair delivered new to Smiths Eagle of Trench in 1947. Three years later its original half-cab ACB body was donated to a pre-war Dennis Lancet and it received this much nicer fully-fronted Metalcraft unit instead. Sister vehicle DUX 654, which received a half-cab Metalcraft body, was withdrawn from use in 1963; '655 remained in service until August 1966 and is currently preserved. (B Mel Gough Collection)

After the Midland Red acquisition of the SOA 'rota' services in April 1978, three of the local operators (H Brown, Martlew and Smiths Britannia) merged into Wrekin Coach Services Ltd, trading as Britannia Travel. Ford R192/Plaxton Derwent bus XUX 417K had been new to another Telford area operator, Hoggins of Wrockwardine Wood, passing to Midland Red in January 1974 and then to Britannia. (B Mel Gough)

Despite the destination blinds these Guy Vixen/ECW buses are a long way from London Transport's Country Area – their livery and the stylised "plucked chicken" logos gave the game away! MXX 364 (fleet number 1, formerly GS64) and MXX 354 (fleet number 2, formerly GS54) came to JP Wood in 1969 and were replaced by minibuses in 1979/80. Both vehicles passed into preservation, albeit in London Transport green. Can we have a preserved GS in another livery please? There are enough of them! (Ted Jones via Chris Warn)